THE WORLD OF
PILGRIMAGE

GEORGE TARGET

AA

CONTENTS

CHRISTIANITY

Produced by AA Publishing © The Automobile Association 1997
Maps © The Automobile Association 1997

All rights reserved. No part of this publication may be reproduced, stored in a retrieval system, or transmitted in any form or by any means – electronic, photocopying, recording or otherwise – unless the written permission of the publishers has been obtained beforehand.

Published by AA Publishing (a trading name of Automobile Association Developments Limited, whose registered office is Norfolk House, Priestley Road, Basingstoke, Hampshire RG24 9NY; registered number 1878835).

ISBN 0 7495 1209 1

A CIP catalogue record for this book is available from the British Library.

The contents of this book are believed correct at the time of printing. Nevertheless, the publishers cannot be held responsible for any errors or omissions or for changes in the details given in this book or for the consequences of any reliance on the information provided by the same. We have tried to ensure accuracy in this book, but things do change and we would be grateful if readers would advise us of any inaccuracies they may encounter.

Copy editors: Karen Kemp, Janet Tabinski, Nia Williams
Picture researcher: Kathy Lockley ❖ Design Grahame Dudley Associates
Colour separation by Daylight Colour Art, Singapore
Printed and in Italy by Tipolitografia G Canale & C SpA – Turin

INTRODUCTION

·

We are the Pilgrims ... we shall go

Always a little further: it may be

Beyond that last blue mountain barred with snow,

Across that angry or that glimmering sea ...

(JAMES ELROY FLECKER, THE GOLDEN JOURNEY TO SAMARKAND)

A PILGRIMAGE IS a journey made for religious reasons usually beyond the call of everyday worship to a place believed to be holy. Even a short journey to a shrine can be a pilgrimage.

There are all manner of reasons for making such a journey: pilgrims may hope to obtain spiritual succour or material benefits from the pilgrimage, perhaps a cure from disease or some other affliction, perhaps the achievement of peace of mind or prosperity, a sense of unity with other like-minded people; or they may be doing penance for their sins, or giving thanks for blessings already received, or simply offering praise or devotion.

Every pilgrimage needs a focal point and there are many such holy places all over the world, both ancient and modern. They may be the remote tops of certain hills or mountains, weathered rocks, lonely caves in the wilderness, small lakes, deep-running rivers, groves of trees, sun-dappled glades deep in the woods or mysterious circles and patterns of standing stones.

Some are holy because a god or goddess may have walked on this earth there, or appeared in a vision to one or more believers, or because holy men and women have lived and prayed and died there, leaving a relic of their days. Convinced of its significance, people have then sought to house this legacy of holiness, be it physical or spiritual, in buildings of wood or stone.

Pilgrimage is an evocative word. Most religions have these places of pilgrimage, some simple and austere, others magnificently embellished structures.

Apart from their beauty or historical interest, why should believers go on a pilgrimage at all? Isn't the idea rather quaint or even superstitious? And what possible relevance can such a journey have for contemporary people?

Perhaps we are in danger of losing our spirituality; perhaps pilgrims, by undertaking such a journey, are seeking to regain it. To go on a pilgrimage is to learn, as William Blake did, how 'to see ... Heaven in a Wild Flower' and to 'Hold Infinity in the palm of your hand' *(Auguries of Innocence)*.

Finding a way through chaos

No place needs to be blessed by priests or approved by politicians to be made holy. Pilgrims who travel to Lourdes, Stonehenge, Santiago de Compostela or the Great Hall of

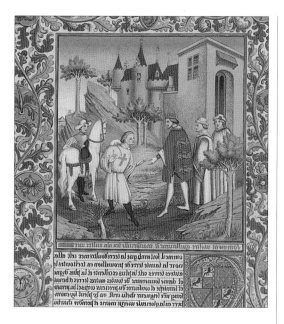

tourist, or with the faith of a pilgrim. Visit any of them as a sceptic, and you will see only what you think you already know – the loss being your own. Remember that beyond the surface of shrines and relics, beneath the mere things of wood and stone, even above the occasional glories of sight and sound, there are intimations of immortality.

Yet even Jesus Christ, whose followers form a spiritual temple, taught in a temple of stone; the Prophet Muhammad commanded pilgrimage to Mecca; and the Lord Krishna and the Lord Buddha smile serenely from a thousand shrines.

By choosing the best days and times, it is still possible to have your deepest emotions touched, to see the light of Heaven through even the worst sentimental stained glass. What you bring with you is almost as important as what is there. Remain open to sight, sound, touch, taste and smell. Don't just watch: take part. Don't be a tourist: celebrate, and discover in faith the real world of a pilgrim.

ABOVE: a modern pilgrim kisses the place of Christ's birth in Nazareth

LEFT: Richard I, the Crusading king, bids bon voyage to a 12th-century pilgrim

OPPOSITE PAGE: a 15th-century illustration of pilgrims leaving Canterbury

the Buddha, seeking the great mystery at the heart of the cosmos, must find their way through the unhappy confusions between religions and reach beyond the barbed wire of political prejudice.

There are two ways to see these holy places of pilgrimage: with the curiosity of a

BELOW: the El Rocio pilgrimage in Spain

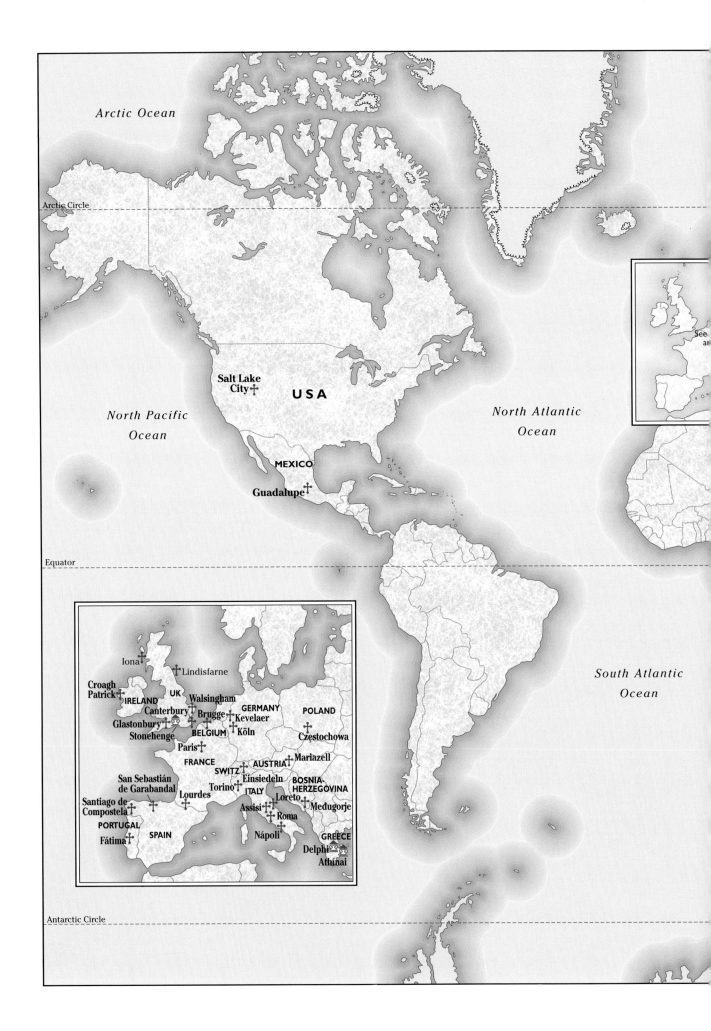

Arctic Ocean

Arctic Circle

North Pacific
Ocean

Salt Lake
City ✝

USA

North Atlantic
Ocean

MEXICO

Guadalupe ✝

See
an

Equator

South Atlantic
Ocean

Iona ✝
✝ Lindisfarne

Croagh
Patrick ✝   UK   Walsingham
    IRELAND ✝ Canterbury ✝ ✝ Brugge   GERMANY   POLAND
Glastonbury ✝ ✝ Kevelaer
Stonehenge   BELGIUM ✝ Köln
                              ✝ Częstochowa
            Paris ✝
            FRANCE   AUSTRIA ✝ Mariazell
          SWITZ ✝ ✝
San Sebastián   ✝ Einsiedeln   BOSNIA-
de Garabandal   Torino ✝ ITALY HERZEGOVINA
            Lourdes ✝   Loreto ✝
Santiago de ✝   Assisi ✝✝ ✝ Medugorje
Compostela   ✝ Roma
PORTUGAL   SPAIN
Fátima ✝   Nápoli ✝   GREECE
                        Delphi ✝✝
                        Athínai

Antarctic Circle

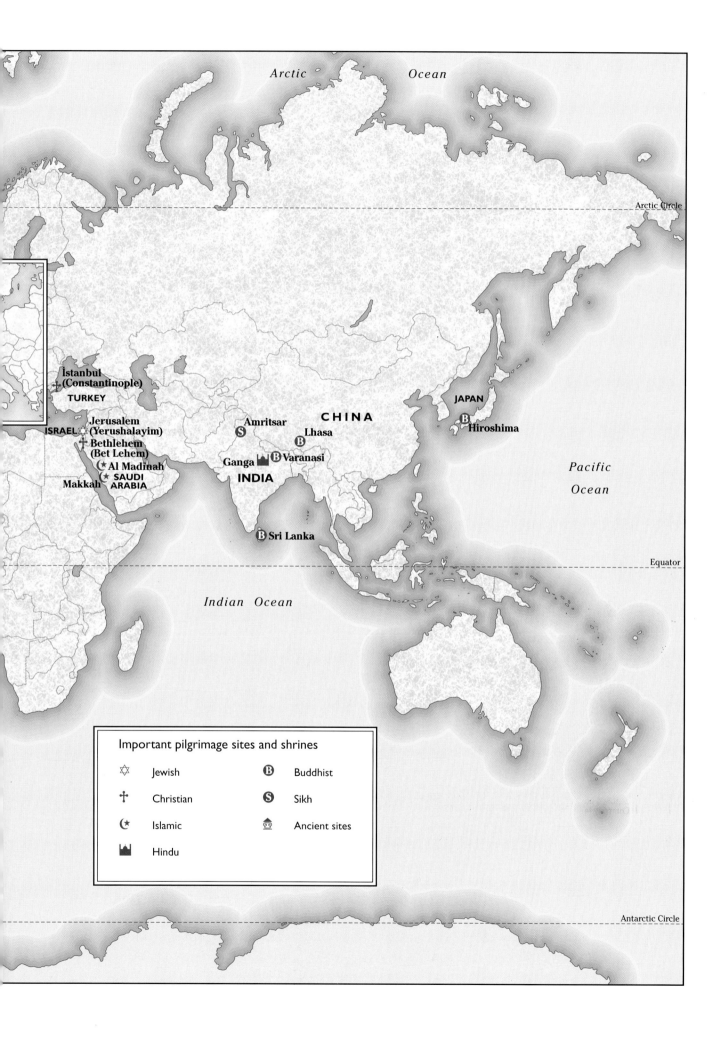

Arctic Ocean

Arctic Circle

İstanbul
(Constantinople)
TURKEY

Jerusalem
(Yerushalayim)
ISRAEL
Bethlehem
(Bet Lehem)
Al Madinah
SAUDI
Makkah ARABIA

Amritsar
S

Ganga
INDIA

CHINA

Lhasa
B

B Varanasi

JAPAN

B
Hiroshima

Pacific

Ocean

Sri Lanka
B

Equator

Indian Ocean

Antarctic Circle

Important pilgrimage sites and shrines

✡ Jewish   B Buddhist

✝ Christian   S Sikh

☾★ Islamic   Ancient sites

Hindu

JERUSALEM

A medieval view of the city of Jerusalem

*J*ERUSALEM IS the largest and most significant mixed pilgrimage of them all. Jews, Christians and Muslims travel here, to the repository of Jewish religious history and present political hopes, where Jesus walked and preached and died, and where Muhammad ascended from the earth for an audience with Allah in Paradise.

For the Jews, Jerusalem (Yerushalayim) was and still is the city of promise: 'Thus saith the Lord, I am returned to Jerusalem with mercies, My house shall be built in it ... And many nations shall come, and say, "Let us go up to the Mountain of the Lord, and to the House of God, for the Law of God and the Word of God shall go forth from Jerusalem"' (The Old Testament, Isaiah II: 1–3).

Christians remember it as the city over which Christ wept: 'O Jerusalem, Jerusalem, which killest the prophets, and stonest them that are sent in judgement unto thee: How often would I have gathered thy children together, as a hen doth gather her brood under her wings – but ye would not!' (The New Testament, Matthew XXIII: 37–8).

Muslims believe that the beautiful golden dome of the mosque on the summit of Mount Moriah, from where Muhammad ascended to the heavens, marks the heart and centre of the world, and is the oldest surviving Islamic building anywhere.

Jerusalem has become the symbol of Paradise, a 'new Heaven and a new Earth, the holy city sent down from God, her light like a stone most precious, even a jasper clear as crystal, her walls great and high, with twelve gates of pearl, and twelve foundations, foursquare, and the city pure gold, garnished with all manner of precious stones ... and we shall walk in the light of it, and shall live in it for ever and ever. Amen' (The New Testament, The Book of Revelation XXI).

Pilgrims of all three faiths have been coming here for over 1,500 years, at first in peace, then as armies engaged in wars over the possession of these holy places. Innumerable lives were sacrificed during the Christian Crusades against the 'heathen hordes' who occupied and claimed the Holy Land in the name of another God.

The Golden String to Paradise

I give you the end of a golden string;
Only wind it into a ball,
It will lead you in at Heaven's gate,
Built in Jerusalem's wall.

(WILLIAM BLAKE, JERUSALEM)

For the medieval pilgrim, that 'golden string' could be picked up in any city, town, village or mud-and-wattle hut in Christendom, and had to be followed on foot or on horseback along crude roads and tracks, through the dark woodland which then covered most of Europe, over rivers and mountains, sometimes by sea, across deserts, travelling day after day, week after week. Today's pilgrims can book at the travel agency, board the plane and leave maps and navigation to the pilot – but their devotion is none the less for that.

Ancient and modern

The Jerusalem of today is really two cities – the old and the new. On the one hand there are gleaming skyscrapers and hotels, armed

police on the streets, the occasional glimpse of a patrolling armoured car; on the other there are scores of churches, towers, minarets and domed mosques, narrow arched alleys, and bazaars and stepped streets between blocks of stone houses, and inner courtyards straight out of the pages of the Old Testament.

Jerusalem was built on the high lands of ancient Judaea, where the nomadic shepherds of the desert met the settled farmers of the Plain of Sharon. This was a place of contact between many peoples and races, armies, traders and migrants.

It has been built and destroyed, neglected, rebuilt and destroyed again, and is now a capital city, a fortress of refuge, an open market and a spiritual home. It was made capital of the Hebrew kingdom in 1000 BC; captured and destroyed by the Babylonians in 586 BC; taken by the Romans and destroyed yet again during the Jewish uprisings of AD 70 and 135; ruled by Arabs, Turks, European crusaders and Egyptians and eventually conquered by the British in 1917.

In 1948 Jerusalem was divided between the Jews, who held the new city, and the Arabs, who took control of the old; the city was unified once again after the Six-Day War of 1967.

Few places are richer in religious association. Despite all the changes that have engulfed it since those beginnings in slaughter and conquest – those tidal waves of defeat and destruction, times of breaking and building, weeping and laughter, mourning and dancing, silence and singing, the burial of historical sites beneath the rubble of generations, the growth of legends – Jerusalem continues to be the most visited of all the pilgrim cities.

ABOVE: Muslim pilgrims surge into Temple Mount, site of the Dome of the Rock, in the Old City

BELOW: the Holy City of Jerusalem today

JERUSALEM
focus for three faiths

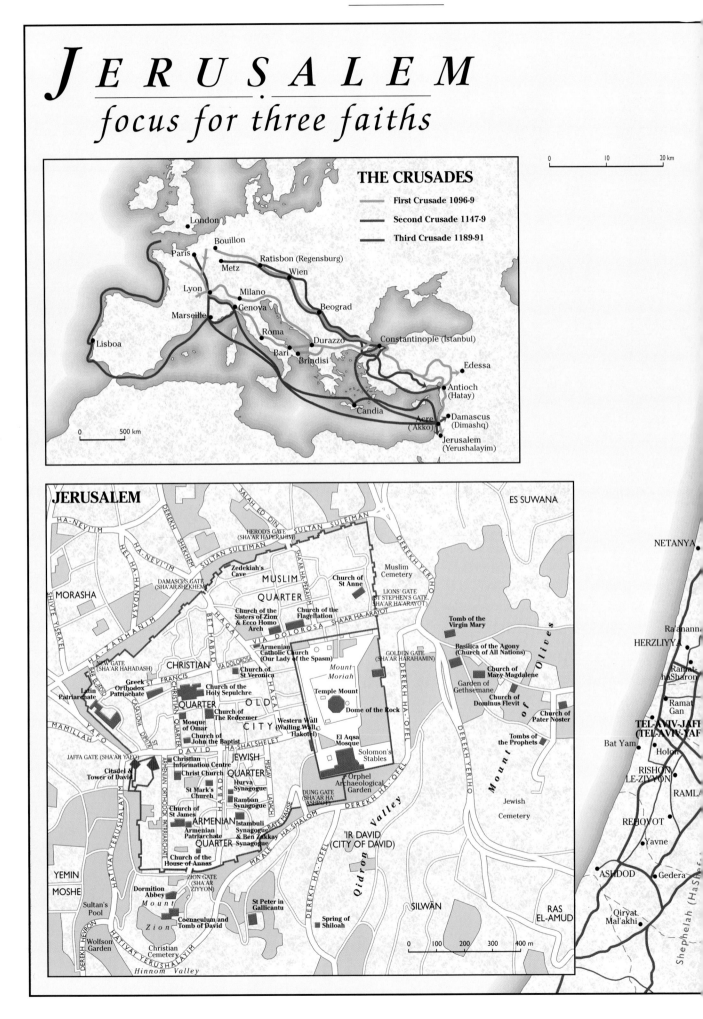

0   10   20 km

THE CRUSADES

— First Crusade 1096-9

— Second Crusade 1147-9

— Third Crusade 1189-91

London

Bouillon

Paris

Ratisbon (Regensburg)

Metz   Wien

Lyon   Milano

Genova

Marseille

Roma

Lisboa   Bari   Brindisi   Durazzo   Constantinople (Istanbul)

Candia

Edessa

Antioch (Hatay)

Acre ('Akko)   Damascus (Dimashq)

Jerusalem (Yerushalayim)

0   500 km

JERUSALEM

ES SUWANA

HA-NEVI'IM

DEREKH SHEKHEM

SALAH ED-DIN

SULTAN SULEIMAN

HEROD'S GATE (SHA'AR HAPERAHIM)

DEREKH YERIHO

HEL HA-HANDASA

HA-NEVI'IM   SULTAN SULEIMAN

MORASHA   DAMASCUS GATE (SHA'AR SHEKHEM)

Zedekiah's Cave   Muslim Cemetery

MUSLIM

Church of St Anne

SHIVTE YISRAEL   QUARTER   LIONS' GATE (ST STEPHEN'S GATE, SHA'AR HA 'ARAYOT)

HA-ZANHANIM   Church of the Sisters of Zion & Ecco Homo Arch   Church of the Flagellation

Tomb of the Virgin Mary

BET HABAD   VIA DOLOROSA   SHA'AR HA-ARAYOT

Armenian Catholic Church (Our Lady of the Spasm)   Basilica of the Agony (Church of All Nations)

NEW GATE (SHA'AR HAHADASH)   VIA DOLOROSA   GOLDEN GATE (SHA'AR HARAHAMIN)

CHRISTIAN   Church of St Veronica

Mount Moriah   Church of Mary Magdalene

Latin Patriarchate   Greek Orthodox Patriarchate   Church of the Holy Sepulchre

Temple Mount   Garden of Gethsemane   Church of Dominus Flevit

QUARTER   OLD   Church of Pater Noster

CASSOVA DMRI.   Church of The Redeemer   CITY

MAMILLAH   Mosque of Omar   Western Wall (Wailing Wall Hakotel)   Dome of the Rock

Church of John the Baptist   HA-SHALSHELET

DEREKH HA-'OFEL   Mount of Olives

JAFFA   Christian Information Centre   JEWISH   El Aqsa Mosque   Tombs of the Prophets

JAFFA GATE (SHA'AR YAFO)   Christ Church   QUARTER   MISGAV   Solomon's Stables

Citadel & Tower of David   Hurva Synagogue   DEREKH HA-'OFEL

St Mark's Church   Ramban Synagogue   Orphel Archaeological Garden

Church of St James   DUNG GATE (SHA'AR HA' ASHPOT)   Jewish Cemetery

ARMENIAN   Istambuli Synagogue & Ben Zakkay Synagogue

Armenian Patriarchate   QUARTER   Qidron Valley

Church of the House of Annas   'IR DAVID (CITY OF DAVID)

YEMIN   ZION GATE (SHA'AR ZIYYON)

MOSHE   Dormition Abbey

Sultan's Pool   Mount   St Peter in Gallicantu

Coenaculum and Tomb of David   SILWAN   RAS EL-AMUD

Zion   Spring of Shiloah

Wolfson Garden

Christian Cemetery

Hinnom Valley

DEREKH HEVRON   HATIVAT YERUSHALAYIM   HA'ALE HA-SHALOM

NETANYA

Ra'anann

HERZLIYYA

Ramat haSharon

Ramat Gan

TEL-AVIV-JAFI (TEL-AVIV-YAF

Bat Yam   Holon

RISHON LE-ZIYYON

RAMLA

REHOVOT

Yavne

ASHDOD   Gedera

Qiryat Mal'akhi

Shephelah (HaShefe

0   100   200   300   400 m

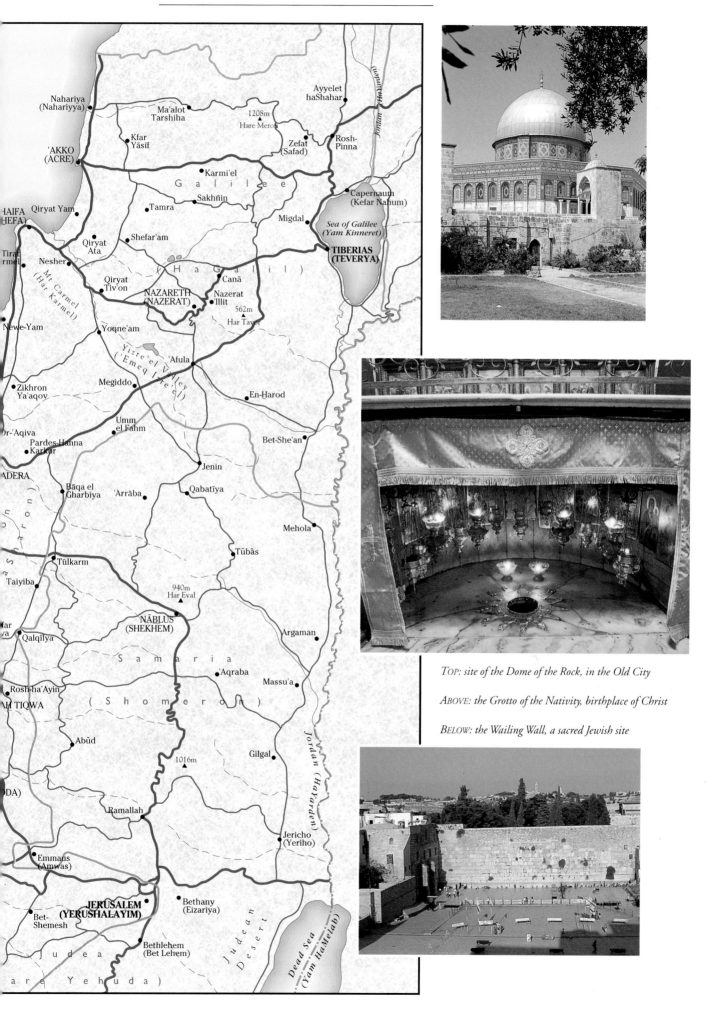

TOP: *site of the Dome of the Rock, in the Old City*

ABOVE: *the Grotto of the Nativity, birthplace of Christ*

BELOW: *the Wailing Wall, a sacred Jewish site*

JEWISH
JERUSALEM

For the Jewish worshipper there is no one particular site of pilgrimage within the city of Jerusalem: the whole place is holy.

ALTHOUGH JEWS REVERE the city as a whole, the pious will not visit Jerusalem without praying at the Western (Wailing) Wall. This tradition began during the years following the destruction of the city and the Jews' temple by the Romans in AD 70, as retribution for the Jewish revolt a generation or so after the death of Jesus. Tens of thousands of men and women were slain or crucified, thousands more were taken into slavery or driven with their children into exile, and the survivors, under penalty of death, were forbidden to return to the ruins. Later, a token few were allowed to make a pilgrimage back to weep over the stones, the very sight of which would be enough to remind them of the futility of revolt. This marked the real beginning of the Jewish tradition of visiting the Western Wall.

A black-attired Jewish man lamenting the sorrows of Israel at the Wailing Wall

Weeping for Israel

After the fall of the Roman Empire the tradition hardened into a formal ritual, which persisted throughout the various Muslim and Christian occupations of Jerusalem. On Yom Kippur, the Day of Atonement (which ends the New Year's period of penitence), pious Jewish men, each dressed in a shroud, would gather among the fallen stones of what they believed was the wall of King Herod's temple and wail over the shattered glories of their fallen and desecrated home.

It has now been established that the huge stones of the present Western Wall actually formed part of the lower supporting foundations of the boundary to the outer court of King Herod's temple at the time of Christ. Some may be the genuine remnants of the original temple which was built by King Solomon, ruler of Israel in the 10th century BC.

The large area in front of this length of towering masonry has been cleared and paved with slabs, and forms a quadrangle in which the lamentations are made. The more accessible surfaces of stone have been worn down to smoothness by the fingers and lips of the devout.

At all hours of the day, and sometimes even during the watches of the night, it is genuinely moving to hear Jewish pilgrims sobbing as they lean their heads against those venerable stones, chanting the Penitential Psalms in Hebrew, and breaking their hearts over the sorrows of Israel.

However, not all rituals at the Western Wall are sorrowful. Jews believe that the Rose of Sharon, praised in the biblical *Song of Solomon* – the bride whose 'belly is like an heap of wheat set about with lilies' and whose breasts are 'like clusters of grapes' – is a

ABOVE: prayers and wishes are noted and left in the crevices of the Western Wall

LEFT: a Bar Mitzvah, marking a boy's progression into adulthood, held at the Western Wall

symbol of the Sabbath. Just before sunset every Friday evening, at the beginning of the Jewish Sabbath, worshippers assemble and read from the *Song of Solomon*, to put themselves in the right spirit for the holy day.

Yad Vashem

All Jewish pilgrims who come to Jerusalem are likely to want to spend time at its other site of sorrows: Yad Vashem, the Hall of Remembrance for the six million who were killed under Nazi rule during the Holocaust.

Built in 1957, it stands on a hill, set away from the daily turmoil of life in the new city, on a vast, barren platform of stark concrete with walls of grey basalt boulders. Inside, a bronze cup holds the eternal flame of remembrance, and the names of the 21 Nazi-run concentration camps are set into the floor. Here, in semi-darkness, the living look upon

the dying, recalled in displays and archives, and weep for those who have no more tears to shed, as they mourn the fate of millions who were sacrificed to an obscene ideology.

Finally the pilgrims emerge into the sunshine of Jerusalem, having paid their homage at a shrine whose relevance to the modern world cannot be doubted.

ABOVE: the victims of tyranny are remembered at Yad Vashem

THE CRUSADES

FOR OVER TWO CENTURIES CRUSADES were a regular feature of medieval life, marching out against pagans or heretics or, in the most spectacular and costly enterprises, against Islam, with the ultimate goal of capturing Palestine, the Holy Land.

IN 1095 POPE URBAN II received a call from the Byzantine Emperor against the Seljuk Turks, and spotted an ideal opportunity to extend Christendom and to distract Europe's large population of warring knights. Urban aroused fervent support for a campaign, promising a general pardon for atrocities committed against the infidel. The zeal of his preachers persuaded 20,000 peasants and labourers to set out for Constantinople, slaughtering Jewish communities on their way. Alarmed by this undisciplined 'People's Crusade', the Emperor shipped his first would-be saviours off to Asia Minor, where they were massacred by Turkish troops.

The First Crusade

It took another year for the official crusade to arrive, many soldiers having sold off their possessions in France, Britain and Italy to fund the journey. Now European military tradition came up against the skills of the Muslim archers. The Christian army's main strategy was brute force: close-knit bodies of heavily armed, mounted knights bulldozing through the opposition. This tactic lost much of its effect as the Muslims fired from the flanks, shooting the knights' horses from under them. Disease, heat and starvation also took their toll on the crusaders, but they had one key advantage: the deep rift between Sunni and Shi'ite Muslims. Weakened by their divisions, the Muslims allowed Christian troops to march into Jerusalem in June 1099, where they proceeded to slaughter its inhabitants.

The Second Crusade

Having captured Jerusalem, the crusaders set up four states: Jerusalem itself, Edessa, Tripoli and Antioch. Together they formed the fortified region of Outremer, protected by religious military orders such as the Knights Templar. Over nearly 50 years the settlers of Outremer and their Muslim neighbours grew to understand each other and new alliances were forged. This period of peace and negotiation was shattered when a tough new generation of ambitious Muslim leaders proclaimed a *jihad* (Holy War) against the Christians and conquered Edessa. The Second Crusade, summoned to the Holy Land in 1147, failed after the abandonment of the siege of Damascus. Within another 40 years Saladin had led Muslim troops into Jerusalem and captured its treasured fragment of the 'True Cross'. The loss of the Holy City sent shock waves through Europe, and was said to have killed Pope Urban III.

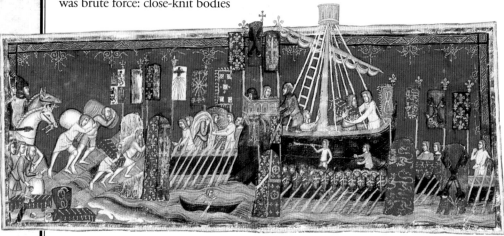

TOP RIGHT: *departure for the Holy Land;* ABOVE: *boats being loaded*

The Third Crusade

Urban's successor, Gregory VIII, rallied the support of three of Europe's most powerful rulers: Frederick Barbarossa, the Holy Roman Emperor; King Philippe Auguste of France, and Richard I, the Lionheart, of England. Frederick led his army into Asia Minor ahead of the others but drowned during a river crossing. In 1190 the rest of the crusade got under way and joined the soldiers already laying siege to the Muslim city of Acre. When the starving citizens finally surrendered, a ransom was demanded. Saladin could not raise the money and Richard I had his prisoners killed, one by one, in full view of the Muslim army.

The Lionheart was an able strategist, keeping his ranks intact as they marched along the coast towards Jerusalem, supplied by his ships and protected by crossbowmen. Nevertheless, two years of fighting failed to win back the Holy City. Richard eventually gave up and returned home, after signing a truce with Saladin, by which pilgrims were allowed access to Jerusalem and the True Cross fragment was returned.

The end of an era

The fourth crusade, in 1202, ran into trouble before starting. A fraction of the expected troops turned up at Venice, leaving those who had answered the call with massive debts to the Venetian bankers who had paid for their ships. To raise the funds they captured a Christian city, Zara, and then headed for Constantinople, where the deposed Emperor's son, Alexius, offered to pay for their support. When Alexius was killed by his own subjects, the crusaders ran riot, carrying off the city's relics and loot.

The Sack of Constantinople made a mockery of the crusaders' original aims; it also left the Byzantine Empire open to the invasions of the Ottoman Turks. By the 14th century even the Holy Land's military orders were feared by European Christians. In 1307 the king of France had all Knights Templar charged with witchcraft. Their Grand Master was burned at the stake and their riches confiscated. The crusading era, violent and often vengeful, had come to a fitting end.

BELOW: the pillage of Jerusalem, 1099

CHRISTIAN JERUSALEM

The Christian pilgrim comes to Jerusalem and the Holy Land to walk where Jesus walked, usually travelling by coach a few kilometres south of Jerusalem to start at the beginning at Bethlehem and the Church of the Nativity.

Bethlehem

From its humble beginnings as the burial place of Rachel, wife of Jacob, nearly 2,000 years BC, Bethlehem slowly grew into the little town where Jesus was born. But the settlement has long since developed beyond its biblical proportions.

The Church of the Nativity, the town's focal point, is built like a fortress, and is probably the oldest Christian building in the world, possibly dating back to the 6th century, though pilgrims have been visiting the site – set in a cave – since at least the 2nd century.

The original basilica was built over a group of caves in 325; the later building may have been the work of Emperor Justinian. The church has a central nave, two rows of columns and, beyond the columns (left and right of the high altar), two flights of steps down to the caves beneath. There, on the

RESPONSIBILITY FOR Jerusalem's holy places is often shared out among the denominations: Roman Catholic, Protestant, Greek Orthodox, Armenian, Syrian, Coptic, Ethiopian or other custodians. Competition between them can sometimes erupt into unseemly behaviour. Recently, Greek Orthodox and Armenian monks fought with broomsticks and chairs over who should control various parts of the Church of the Nativity, and the incident was quelled by riot police.

RIGHT: the Grotto of the Nativity

RIGHT: Christians queue to be baptised in the waters of the River Jordan, near the Sea of Galilee

RIGHT: Christians queue to be baptised in the waters of the River Jordan, near the Sea of Galilee

floor of the Grotto of the Nativity, set in cracked marble, is a 14-pointed silver star and the Latin inscription: *Hic de Virgine Maria Jesus Christus natus est* ('Here was Jesus Christ born of the Virgin Mary').

Hewn out of the nearby rock face, lined in more marble, is the manger in which the swaddled baby Jesus is said to have lain; it is now lit with 15 golden lamps and glimmering candles and viewed by crowds of pilgrims, tourists, guides and monks. Some visitors are visibly moved; others often break into joyous song.

CENTRE: the Church of the Nativity

Nazareth

Coaches travel the 100km north from Jerusalem to Nazareth, through awe-inspiring scenery of the mountain passes of Samaria. Jesus grew up in Nazareth, 'waxed strong in spirit', was 'subject unto his parents,' and 'increased in wisdom and stature, and in favour with God and man' (The New Testament, Luke II).

His home would have been much like any of the basic dwellings you can still see among the olive trees: wattle and daub, low and square, probably with two rooms – one for the family and one for the goats and sheep. But this Holy House has been transported to

Loreto, in Italy (see pages 42–4). The real purpose of a pilgrimage to Nazareth is to walk where Jesus calmed the waters and won disciples from among the fishermen – by the Sea of Galilee.

The ancient city of Tiberias, on its western shore, a hotch-potch of Herodian ruins and Crusader castles, old stone and new buildings, has a pleasant, convivial air, with its waterfront promenade, swaying palms and strolling crowds. Yet walk away from all that for only a few minutes and there are the dark waters, the nets of the fishermen, and the place where Jesus told his disciples to 'come, follow me'.

The Way of the Cross

Pilgrims who follow Jesus back through the Holy Land to Jerusalem find that the land-

WHEN VISITING HOLY PLACES, a reverent pilgrim may encounter people whose attitude is less than sensitive. For example, in his book *Where Jesus Walked* (Stanborough Press 1986), writer David Marshall describes his visit to the Church of the Nativity, at the same time as a large group of white-robed Nigerian nuns. As the nuns knelt in devotion around the star, an American woman nudged her husband: 'Hey! They're praying! Get a shot of them, George, while they're praying!' In cases like this, the Christian virtues of patience and forgiveness are undoubtedly called for.

LEFT: the nave and
altar of the Church
of the Nativity

scape is much altered since biblical times. Where, exactly, did he fast for 40 days and 40 nights in the wilderness? On the side of which hill did he preach the Sermon on the Mount?

But there are nevertheless many sites and relics that are claimed to be authentic survivors from the time of Christ: the village where the Marriage Feast of Cana was held, complete with the six stone jars in which the water was changed into wine; wells from which he must have drunk; roads along which he undoubtedly walked; and even fragments from the five barley loaves and two small fishes with which he fed the five thousand.

The village of Bethany, a day's journey out of Jerusalem, where Jesus often stayed at the house of Mary and Martha, has disappeared under new buildings – but the foundations of the house and the stones of the low tomb of Lazarus can be visited.

In Jerusalem itself, the temple where he taught was destroyed completely in the 1st century. The Garden of Gethsemane, where he knelt in prayer before his arrest, is flanked by roads and walled in on three sides, most of it enclosed on the fourth side by the 20th-century Basilica of the Agony (built on the site of several earlier versions). But there is enough left for pilgrims to follow Jesus' route to the cross, from the Last Supper to his burial in Joseph of Arimathea's new tomb hewn out of the rock.

The Last Supper

Jesus' last meal with his disciples was held in a 'large upper room furnished and prepared for the Passover meal' (The New Testament, Mark XIV: 15–16; Luke XXII: 12–13); the place is shown to pilgrims in what used to be the Basilica of Holy Zion (Coenaculum). In the 3rd century, long after the whole area had

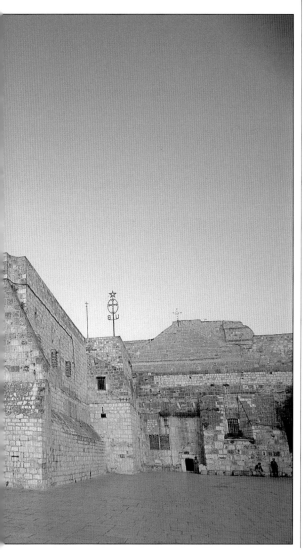

LEFT: the Tomb of Lazarus
in Bethany, 5km from
Jerusalem. Lazarus, raised
from the dead by Jesus, is
revered by Muslims as well
as Christians

ABOVE: the 'large upper room' said to be the site of the Last Supper

been destroyed by the Romans, a small chapel was built over the traditional site of the house. A century later this chapel was incorporated into the basilica then being erected – which was subsequently burnt down, once by the Persians and twice by the Muslims, and eventually restored by the Crusaders. Then, under the Turks, control of the basilica passed to the Muslims, who venerated the site as the burial place of King David, and it was converted into a mosque.

Since the Six-Day War of 1967, the site has been in the possession of the Jews, who venerate this tomb of David as one of the holiest places in Israel – though they do allow Christian and Muslim access.

The upper room is a large, vaulted chamber above the old chapel, with rather heavy-looking columns of porphyry, whose capitals are carved with symbolic bunches of grapes and ears of wheat in memory of the bread and wine taken at the Last Supper. This is also thought to be the same upper room where the Holy Spirit descended in 'cloven tongues like as of fire' on the disciples at the Feast of Pentecost (The New Testament, Acts II: 2–4).

The Garden of Gethsemane

After the Last Supper, Jesus and his disciples went out to the Mount of Olives, now land-marked during the day as the environs of the International Hotel, and floodlit by night. They came to a place where there was a garden, called Gethsemane, and Jesus told his disciples that his soul was 'very sorrowful, even unto death', and prayed to his Father three times that this hour might pass from him – 'Nevertheless, not as I will, but as Thou wilt'. Three times he returned to his disciples, and found them sleeping, and asked them: 'Could ye not watch with me one hour?' Then came his arrest: 'Behold, the hour is at hand, and the Son of man is betrayed into the hands of sinners' (The New Testament, Matthew XXVI: 36–46).

By night the present Garden of Gethsemane (the name means 'oil press') is closed except for special services. By day, once they have passed along Palm Sunday Lane and into the basilica, what pilgrims are shown is all rather too neat and tidy to convey any impression of the anguish Jesus suffered there: flowers form a carpet beneath the olive trees, and bougainvillaea and honeysuckle trail over the walls. The eight gnarled olive trees, say the Franciscan guides, are the very same that witnessed the agony – which is an awe-inspiring thought in itself.

Inside the basilica itself, the Rock of Agony is candle-lit for veneration, and many pilgrims prostrate themselves before it. An underground chapel, with purple stained glass, hundreds of candles and the warmth and pungency of burning wax, is claimed to occupy the actual site where Christ prayed.

Arrest and trial

Jesus was seized at Gethsemane by a band of armed men and soldiers from the High Priest and elders of the people, taken to Caiaphas, the High Priest, and accused of blasphemy, amid blows, mockery and spitting, and then bound and delivered to Pontius Pilate, the Roman Procurator (or Governor) of Judaea. This would have been at the Antonia Tower or Fortress, set against the northern outer wall of the temple compound and dominating it.

The whole area was flattened during the Roman destruction of Jerusalem, and event-

IN ONE CORNER of the temple courtyard the Pavement is scored with the marks of games played by Roman soldiers: knuckle-bones, hopscotch and the 'circle game'. This was played with lettered stones, and had moves such as Alexander's Step, the Ephebos and the King's Gambit. It has been suggested that Jesus might have been dragged there and made the butt of such a game: 'the King's Gambit for the King of the Jews'.

ually built over by the Convent of the Catholic Sisters of Zion, but recent excavations have unearthed remains of the huge foundations, and a large interior courtyard paved with great stone slabs. The Bible states that Pilate 'sat down on the judgement seat at a place called the Pavement, and in Hebrew, Gab'batha' (The New Testament, John XX: 13–14), and that Jesus stood before him to be questioned and tried. There are no remains of the Scala Santa, or Holy Stairs, which Jesus ascended to face Pilate, as these were taken to Rome by St Helena early in the 4th century, where they are still venerated in the Church of San Giovanni in Laterano (see page 77).

However, the Pavement, carefully preserved, is now inside the walls of the convent, so it is possible to see the very stones on which Jesus stood: slabs of granite and limestone, crossed by gutters and drains, pitted, rutted, grooved by the wheels of chariots, cut with sockets for posts and the standards of the Roman Legions, and worn smooth by millions of feet over the years. There, Pilate 'found no fault in him' – but, fearing the wrath of the Jews, had him scourged and then crucified.

The Via Dolorosa

After the scourging and the mocking, Jesus carried his cross along the Via Dolorosa – 'Way of Sorrows'. Now, every Friday afternoon during the tourist season, pilgrims travel along contemporary streets, between the place of judgement and Golgotha, the 'place of the skull', where Jesus was crucified. The Good Friday procession is the most impressive. Thousands assemble at the Church of St Anne.

LEFT: pilgrims follow the route to the crucifixion along the Via Dolorosa

ABOVE: the chapel at the third Station of the Cross

To the mourning women Jesus said, 'Daughters of Jerusalem, do not weep for me' (Luke XXIII: 28). The Stations of the Cross are not intended to be a sad devotion, for if the Passion of Christ is a way of pain, it is also seen by Christians as a path of hope leading to certain victory. The idea began when Christian access to Jerusalem was prevented by the various Muslim occupations, and pilgrims who had been there originated an oral tradition as a substitute. Monks and scribes then made the stories real by illustrating them as sequences in hand-written gospels, as paintings on the walls of churches, and eventually as groups of statues around their cloisters. By the 15th century the Franciscans had developed the devotion into much the ritual it is today, though the final selection of incidents was not absolutely settled until the 19th century. There are now 14 stations, or 'stopping places,' each representing one of the traditional incidents on the Way of the Cross – sometimes a painting, sometimes a relief carving, often a group of statues – usually inside a church, but sometimes out of doors. In front of each one, pilgrims stop to meditate or pray. Some are incidents mentioned in the gospels, while others are derived from ancient traditions.

ABOVE RIGHT: the Chapel of the Crucifixion in the Church of the Holy Sepulchre, where pilgrims arrive after travelling the Way of the Cross

OPPOSITE: the Church of the Holy Sepulchre INSET: Greek Orthodox Christians celebrate Easter outside the church

A volunteer, picked by lot each year, bears a small, plain cross. Several churchmen are in attendance: Roman Catholic, Greek Orthodox and Protestant; the atmosphere is subdued, anxious, curious and even nervous.

The procession moves amid all the vitality of Jerusalem, with its evocative smells of over-ripe fruit, new leather, spiced cooking, expensive perfume and bad drains, and its confusion of sounds: the prayers of the priests at intervals, footfalls, distant traffic, the sudden amplified call of the muezzin summoning faithful Muslims to the worship of Allah. A left turn takes the pilgrims through a bazaar, past alleys with lines of washing on dragging loops, towards the square in front of the Church of the Holy Sepulchre.

Pilgrims have followed the Way of the Cross since the 4th century, but, given Jerusalem's destruction, various rebuildings and changes, the route can only be an approximation. Even so, it is possible that the pilgrims are walking on the same stones as Christ, at least for part of the Way. Huge paving slabs, once part of the Roman street, have been excavated and raised to form part of today's route.

The original journey to Golgotha can have been barely a thousand paces 'nigh unto the city'. But it is the devotional aspect of the journey, rather than its historical accuracy, which gives spiritual value for a pilgrim – a sense that to walk in the footsteps of Christ, carrying one's own cross, is to be close to the son of God who died 2,000 years ago.

THE CHURCH OF THE HOLY SEPULCHRE

At the end of the Way of the Cross there is a building that has been demolished several times over the centuries, only to be rebuilt and embellished in many hybrid styles. Nowadays the Church of the Holy Sepulchre is made up of an irregular collection of chapels, shrines and alcoves, each of which belongs to the various Christian denominations around the world.

At the entrance, to the right, steps lead to one of the traditional sites of Golgotha, one half of the small chapel being maintained in comparative simplicity by Roman Catholic

ABOVE: worshippers in the Church of the Holy Sepulchre washing the priest's feet at Easter BELOW: a priest at one of the church's shrines

Franciscan monks, the other by Greek Orthodox priests, whose altar is a blaze of red votive lamps and candle-lit icons. Under this altar there is a brass-ringed hole set in the marble floor, through which pilgrims can touch the actual rock beneath it. According to the guide book, this marks the spot where the cross was inserted into a socket.

Come out into the main Greek Orthodox church, and look left at the horseshoe of black columns around the circular shrine of Christ's tomb, with its suspended lamps and chandeliers and hundreds of candles. There, in the reddish glow beneath the great vaulted roof, is the shrine. Pilgrims go down a well-worn flight of steps and enter through a low doorway. Apart from the priest, there is room only for five or six people at a time.

The sepulchre itself is encased in ornately carved mahogany, and a marble slab covers the stone inside. At the back you are allowed

ABOVE: Golgotha seen from the Garden Tomb
LEFT: an Easter procession in Jerusalem

by another (Coptic) priest to crawl forward one at a time and touch the rock wall. Several other chapels are guarded by Armenian monks – the crypt in which St Helena found the True Cross (see pages 38–9), for example. The darkness of centuries is counterbalanced by the warm blaze of candles and lamps, the potent fragrance of incense and the bright gleam of gold.

THE ALTERNATIVE TOMB

There is a second location where some Christians maintain Jesus was buried, in a garden not far away, called the Garden Tomb. In 1883 General Gordon of Khartoum suggested that this ancient rock-cut tomb was the real place where Jesus was laid to rest, and many pilgrims prefer its simplicity to the Byzantine grandeur of the shrine in the church. The ancient quarried slope in which it is set does look rather like a skull, making it an appropri-

ate setting to take the name of Golgotha (see page 21); and a groove which has been cut into the ground before the entrance may well indicate the rolling of a 'great stone' to block access to the tomb. For many pilgrims, this site in its simplicity evokes a sense of historical Resurrection more effectively than the Church of the Holy Sepulchre.

AFTER THE RESURRECTION, Jesus appeared to his disciples several times: first to Mary Magdalene, then when he walked with two of them on the way to Emmaus, and then while they sat down to eat, and so on. Perhaps most moving was his appearance at the Sea of Galilee, where the disciples had gone fishing to start earning a living again. They fished all night, and in the morning saw Jesus standing on the shore, where a wood fire was burning, with fish cooking on it and bread prepared. Today, one of the waterside restaurants along the shore of Galilee serves a dish called 'St Peter's fish'.

MUSLIM JERUSALEM

·

Celebrated be the praises of Him who took His servant a journey by night from the Sacred Mosque to the Farthest Mosque, the precinct of which we have blessed, to show Him of our signs!

(QU'RAN XVII:1)

The Dome of the Rock

The Dome of the Rock is the most sumptuous holy place in all Jerusalem – perhaps one of the most beautiful buildings in the world. It is on a site revered by Jewish, Christian and Muslim worshippers, and which brings together a wealth of religious association. Up there, at the southern end of the platform of natural rock, King Solomon built his temple to house the Ark of the Covenant, the holiest symbol of God's presence among the Hebrews, a thousand years before Jesus. This was destroyed by the Babylonians four centuries later, but King Herod the Great extended the platform and built his even more impressive temple – only for it to be destroyed by the Romans, about 30 years after the crucifixion of Jesus.

The Dome of the Rock

What the Romans could not destroy was the enormous slab of rock which dominated the platform. To the Jewish worshippers this rock was the place on Mount Moriah, believed by some to be the centre of the world, where Abraham, the Father of Israel, had been willing to sacrifice his own son Isaac in order to demonstrate his trust in Yahweh.

To the Muslims this is the very rock to which the Prophet Muhammad was brought on his Night Journey from the Sacred Mosque (the Ka'bah) in Mecca to the mysterious al-Aqsa, or 'Farthest Mosque'. The Angel Jibril (Gabriel) had roused him from sleep, sat him on a winged beast, half donkey and half mule, and galloped him to Jerusalem. There, a ladder descended, and Jibril took Muhammad up to a door in Heaven – though, before being allowed in, he was also shown the place of Hell: its lid was removed, and he could see the sufferings of the sinners in the awful flames. In Heaven Muhammad met Jesus and John the Baptist, then the Patriarchs Joseph, Moses and Abraham and, finally, he had an audience with Allah, Holy is His Name, who entrusted him with the Five Commands of Islam. The Night Journey and Ascent (*Laylat ul-Isra wal Mi'raj*) of Muhammad is a focal point of Islamic belief, and is commemorated by many Muslims in a whole night of prayer.

At the end of the 7th century the Muslims conquered Jerusalem and uncovered the Rock of Ascent from the rubble, and the Caliph of Damascus had the octagonal Mosque built over it as a shrine of pilgrimage, with the outside covered in gold mosaics. Later, under the administration of the Ottoman Turks, these were replaced by the present Persian tiles in dazzling shades of brilliant blue, clear white and intense green.

The magnificent dome is topped by the proud Crescent of Islam, which can be seen from all over Jerusalem. Though originally of gold, it is now gold-plated, and calligraphic verses from the Qu'ran are an integral part of the glorious decoration around the building.

Inside are towering columns and complicated arabesques, and pilgrims are shown the Holy Rock, with its two footprints of the Prophet Muhammad. In a reliquary on one of the columns, there are hairs from the Prophet's beard.

Although the Dome of the Rock is a place of shared pilgrimage, with the Jewish Wailing Wall set almost immediately beneath it, it is also a symbol of the desperate divisions between Jews and Muslims. Jewish fundamentalists are eager to build a new and even more resplendent temple up on the platform of rock – which would mean that the Dome of the Rock would have to go.

Several times, over recent years, attempts have been made to destroy it: an extreme right-wing Israeli party planned to bomb it in 1982, but was caught by security forces; members of a Jewish fundamentalist sect climbed the wall of the Old City in 1984, and were proceeding to the Dome with explosives when a guard spotted them; and in the same year 20 men were accused in an Israeli court of plotting to blow up the Dome as a prelude to clearing the way for the new temple. They were supported by Christian fundamentalists, who see the rebuilding of the temple as the necessary fulfilment of prophecy before the Second Coming of Jesus Christ – all of which make for dangerous and disturbing times for pilgrims wishing to reaffirm their faith.

BELOW: the Holy Rock, where Muhammad left his footprints as he ascended into Heaven

CHRISTIANITY

T HE HOLY LAND will always be the foremost place of pilgrimage for Christians, but there are many significant sites around the world which draw believers. They are places associated with saints, martyrs and miracles, where the faithful come to pay homage and gain inspiration.

The shrine in the Church of the Holy Sepulchre in Jerusalem, where Jesus died on the cross

RELICS OF CHRIST

ABOVE: Charlemagne, an enthusiastic relic-collector

THE WORD 'RELIC' is derived from the Latin for 'remains' – things that are left behind, especially by a person. 'Reliquary' means a container for such a relic – usually an ornately decorative box or similar container, made so that the relic inside can be seen or displayed for veneration. Religious relics are mostly the portable remains, small surviving scraps of a holy person or his or her belongings. Followers of the world's major religions have always been drawn, with more or less intensity, to the relics of their faith.

The longing for material, tangible items from the past, particularly when linked with our strongest beliefs, is a part of human nature. Within a century of Christ's death the cult of the relic had begun, initially focused on recent martyrs. Remains, reverently cherished, soon acquired miraculous, even magical powers – to cure illnesses and infertility, to ensure a good crop, to grant prosperity or success. In time, relics were being fought over, stolen, bought and sold, and divided into smaller and smaller pieces – either for immense profit or in the pious belief that it was a good thing to spread such remains around to as many churches as possible.

OPPOSITE PAGE: a reliquary holding one of the innumerable holy thorns. This one is kept at the British Museum in London

The prominent place relics have held in the minds of Christians for so many centuries can be difficult for the modern, scientifically orientated mind to comprehend. Today's world demands verifiable evidence of authenticity to go beyond its innate scepticism in such matters, and can only look with disdain on what it sees as the gullibility of the largely illiterate population of the past whose faith blinded them to facts.

Yet the real value of a relic lies not in its authenticity, but rather in its ability to lead a person's heart to the love and mercy of God, through physical reminders of Jesus Christ and the great saints. At the most profound level, the authenticity of a particular relic is in a sense irrelevant as long as the encounter with it results in a step forward on the journey of conversion.

Today's pilgrim is faced with the task of finding a middle way between too much uncritical fervour and a scornful rejection of relics as pious nonsense or deliberate fraud. In a sense, after all, the whole of the Holy Land is itself a relic: the remains of the past preserved in the reliquary of the present.

In the case of Jesus Christ, the possibility of physical remains was limited – the New

A PILGRIMAGE TO THE tomb of the martyred St Thomas à Becket was the device used in Geoffrey Chaucer's *Canterbury Tales* (1387) to bring together an entertaining yet believable mix of personalities from every station in medieval life. While human weakness and sins are shrewdly observed in his characters (the greedy Pardoner, for instance, unrepentently sells 'pigs' bones and ragged bits of cloth' as genuine 'relics of Holy Saints and Martyrs'), the author nevertheless views his pilgrims with a measure of affection to soften his satirical bite.

ABOVE: the Basilica of the Holy Blood in Brugge

Testament relates that on the third day after his crucifixion he rose from the dead and, 40 days later, ascended bodily into Heaven. Although there were a few brief hours of opportunity between his death and his entombment, the idea of salvaging parts of Jesus' body for veneration would have been repugnant to his disciples, who as Jews accorded the greatest respect to dead bodies, and in any case, under Mosaic law, would have rendered themselves ritually unclean by contact with any part of a corpse. Since Jesus left no body behind, most of the relics connected with him are to do with his Passion and death.

Tears in crystal

The gospels record that Jesus wept at his raising of Lazarus from the dead, and over the fate of Jerusalem. Possession of one or more of his teardrops has been claimed by a long list of monasteries, churches and cathedrals which had one or more of these holy tears – usually, like many such relics, brought back from the Holy Land by the Crusaders. The most famous was held by the Benedictines in the Church of the Holy Trinity, Vendôme, which continually trembled in its diamond-set crystal chalice, and attracted immense crowds of pilgrims during the Middle Ages. It was looted at the time of the French Revolution, recovered at the beginning of the 19th century and given into the safe keeping of the Papal Legate, and has not been heard of since.

Agony in Gethsemane

The gospel of St Luke describes the anguished praying of Jesus on the Mount of Olives, when he sweated copiously. Joseph of Arimathea is said to have brought one of the first crystal phials of this sacred sweat to Glastonbury in England (see pages 118–19).

During the Crusades quantities of what was claimed to be Jesus' blood reached Constantinople, and drops were soon being revered at Mantua, and in Rome at Santa Croce, Santa Maria Maggiore and San Giovanni Laterano. Then some reached France

THE MOST RECENT EXAMPLE of an acquired holy foreskin was at the parish church of Calcata, in the Province of Viterbo, about 50km north of Rome. It was called the Carne Vera Santa, or Real Holy Flesh, and venerated on the Feast of the Circumcision every year. Unfortunately, it was stolen in 1983 – probably for the value of its antique silver reliquary – though the parishioners alleged that Rome, disapproving of the veneration, had organised the theft. 'The Church,' said the local bishop, 'would prefer it not to be discussed.'

and England, with Henry III carrying the wondrous relic to Westminster Abbey. The Cistercians at Hailes Abbey in Gloucestershire rebuilt the east end of their abbey church to make it worthy of the treasure which had been authenticated by Pope Urban IV, and the shrine soon became one of the most renowned centres of pilgrimage in the whole of England. However, the abbey was looted by Protestant reformers in the 16th century and the contents of the phial were declared a fake.

Drops traditionally said to be Christ's blood can be revered to this day in the Basilica of the Holy Blood in Brugge, Belgium. The Patriarch of Jerusalem presented them to a Crusader, Count Thierry d'Alsace; upon his return he had a chapel built to house the relic. Although the great 13th-century theologian Thomas Aquinas expressed his doubts about the relic's authenticity, by the 14th century it was said to 'liquefy every Friday between the early morning and the ninth hour'. At the beginning of the 17th century it was held in a crystal tube, sealed at either end with a jewelled crown, and provided with a large, solid silver canopied reliquary. It is now exposed to public view every Friday of the year and throughout the entire week of Ascensiontide. On special Feast Days of the Blood, it is offered to be kissed by pilgrims: a small tube of crystal containing the lamb's wool used to clean Christ's wounds before his burial, and which still appears to be saturated.

The procession of this holy blood through the streets of Brugge on Ascension Thursday, with the relic carried in its magnificent gold and silver reliquary, a metre high and encrusted with diamonds and other precious stones, is the city's most popular tourist attraction. Colourful tableaux are drawn by on floats, and medieval costumes are worn, making a dramatic sight against the background of one of the best-surviving medieval towns in Europe.

The crown of thorns

In the course of his Passion and death, Jesus was crowned with thorns, nailed to a cross and pierced by a spear, and there are many relics representing this sequence of events.

The thorn bushes so common in Isreal would easily have provided the Roman soldiers with the makings of a mock crown, which could conceivably have had between 20 and 40 thorns. Over the centuries, at least 150 churches have claimed to possess one of these thorns, which would seem to throw doubt on the authenticity of some of them at least. One possible explanation for the proliferation is that the original thorns were cut into numerous pieces to allow wider distribution.

Whatever the explanation, miraculous, mundane or simply fraudulent, there are many places where one or more may be revered (the Passion Chapel of Santa Croce in Rome has two). The best-known, at Notre-Dame in Paris, purportedly started out as the whole crown, was sold in the 13th century to the French King Louis IX by the Emperor of Constantinople, and is now a bundle of dried reeds in a circle, without a single remaining thorn, displayed in a ring of six pieces of crystal held together by three gilt leaves. It is offered for veneration on Good Friday.

TOWARDS THE END of the 16th century, in Elizabethan England, a certain John Alleyn was selling 'Christ's blood' to the faithful at £20 a drop – a huge amount of money in those days.

BELOW: Santa Maria Maggiore in Rome: one of the proud possessors of Christ's holy blood

ABOVE: Notre Dame in Paris. The crown of thorns is said to have been brought here – but it has now shed all its thorns

Veronica's veil

After the ordeal of his crowning and scourging, while Jesus was carrying the burden of his cross to Calvary, an ancient tradition tells that a woman, filled with compassion for him, wiped his face with a cloth or kerchief 'on which was left the imprint of his holy countenance' and this cloth is another famous relic. Known as the Vernicle, or Veronica's veil, it was a fragile piece of silk bearing the features of a man. Once it was the most celebrated object of veneration in all Rome, and public exhibitions were great occasions for mass repentance.

The name Veronica comes from two Greek words, meaning 'true' and 'icon' or 'image': hence the woman's name, created around the 15th century to suit the circumstances, was derived from the nature of the

OPPOSITE PAGE: St Veronica displays the imprint of Christ's face on her veil in a 15th-century painting by Hans Memling

THE MOST ORNATELY BEAUTIFUL reliquary for a holy thorn can be found in the Department of Medieval Antiquities at the British Museum in London. The thorn itself is rather inconspicuous, but the jewelled shrine is a wonder of the goldsmith's art, incorporating a cabochon sapphire, pearls and other gems, all in a golden setting of the Passion of Christ, His Second Coming, and the Last Judgement.

relic. Early this century the veil was examined. On the reliquary was the painting of a bearded man, which might have been an interpretation of the miraculous image on the relic itself.

Inside was a square piece of cloth. On this cloth, yellow with age, were two rust-brown stains – perhaps remnants of Christ's blood or sweat but, disappointingly, with no discernible image of a face to reinforce the relic's reputation.

The holy nails

The nails which were used to pierce Jesus' hands and feet on the cross are claimed today by at least 29 different places in Europe alone. Venice, for example, lays claim to three, and Eton College, in England, has four. Of any number of explanations for such a high count, many surrounded by legend, one holds that St Helena, mother of Emperor Constantine and an indefatigable relic-hunter who discovered the True Cross and four holy nails in Jerusalem (see page 36), had the nails made into 12 of smaller size. One of these she is said to have thrown into the Adriatic Sea in order to calm a storm on her journey home; another was incorporated into the head of a statue of her son, Constantine. He used another for decoration on his helmet and body armour, another fashioned into the hilt of his sword, another into a bit for his horse, and sent yet another as a gift to Russia – where it can still be seen in Moscow at the Synod of the Ascension.

Another explanation is that new nails could have been sanctified by dropping a few filings from the original articles into the molten metal. The holy nail at Santa Croce in Rome has certainly been filed. It has even been claimed that new holy nails were produced simply by touching them with an original nail.

In any case, the unique prestige and divine association of these nails appealed to Napoleon. He chose to be crowned King of Italy with the Crown of Theodolinda, which made use of fragments from a holy nail brought to Europe in the 6th century by Pope Gregory the Great.

The True Cross

The True Cross was discovered in the 4th century by St Helena. She found the cross in Jerusalem (see pages 38–9); it bore the superscription 'King of the Jews' at the top. St Helena also discovered the four holy nails, the holy lance and the crosses on which the two thieves had been crucified. These relics were divided and distributed all over Christendom.

St Helena kept the part of the crossbeam most stained with holy blood, and gave the rest to the church at Jerusalem. Within 50 years St Cyril observed that 'the whole world is filled with fragments' (John Calvin was to complain much later that 'if all the pieces were collected into a single heap they would make a good ship-load'). Bits were bought and sold at huge profits, and kings and popes used them as gifts or favours. St Helena's gift to Jerusalem was kept there until Saladin, Sultan of Egypt and Syria, finally defeated the Crusaders in 1187, when it was lost for ever. But enough remained at Constantinople, Cyprus, Antioch, Crete, Edessa, Georgia,

BELOW: Santiago de Compostela, one of the cathedrals in possession of a holy foreskin

Alexandria, Ascalon and Damascus. Santa Croce in Rome had three pieces, one of the holy nails and the superscription, and even the remote Cluniac Priory of St Andrew at Broomeholme, in Norfolk, has a piece which is claimed to have worked many miracles.

The holy lance

Jews were forbidden by religious laws to allow the body of Jesus to hang on the cross into the Sabbath, which would have been a desecration. So Pilate consented to have the legs of Jesus and the two thieves broken, hastening death, as they would be unable to raise themselves in the struggle for breath.

The soldiers broke the legs of the other two, but seeing that Jesus was already dead, one soldier stabbed his spear upwards into Jesus' side to be certain, according to orders. This soldier, mentioned in the gospel of John (the only Evangelist present at the crucifixion), was later given a name, Gaius Cassius Longinus (a corruption of *lonche*, Greek for

(The hammer-headed nail is said to be one of the holy nails, added at some later date.)

From time to time a superstition has been promoted among non-believers that whoever is in possession of the Spear of Destiny, and fully understands its power, holds the world's fate in his or her hands. The superstition has fostered a number of horror stories and has led to much fervent speculation involving such diverse issues as the Book of Revelation, the secret occult activities of Adolf Hitler, the whole history of evil-doing from Golgotha to the years of the Holocaust and to the dropping of the atomic bomb, the search for the Holy Grail, the number of the Beast and, of course, the coming of the Anti-Christ.

Remnants of divinity?

Numerous churches claim to hold relics of Jesus' body, acquired mainly in the heyday of relic veneration. There are records of Christ's hair and fingernail clippings as well as several milk teeth said to have been put aside by his mother when he was little and preserved as keepsakes of his childhood. In the 8th century Charlemagne is supposed to have come into possession of Jesus' navel, which the emperor generously cut into pieces as gifts to Pope Leo and various religious orders.

Until relatively recent times, there was a widespread cult of the holy foreskin, with 13 European churches and cathedrals claiming genuine circumcised foreskins of the infant Jesus, including Santiago de Compostela in Spain, Coulombs and Charroux in France, and the church of San Giovanni Laterano in Rome. Such was the reputation of these relics that the one at Coulombs was lent to King Henry V of England to ensure his wife Catherine's safe delivery of the future Henry VI.

Many contemporary church authorities are genuinely embarrassed about such matters which, they say, bring worthier relics into disrepute and encourage irreverent curiosity.

LEFT: a detail from the Treasury of the Basilica di San Marco in Venice, whose prized relics have included a piece of Mary's veil, some of her hair and milk, one of the holy nails and drops of holy blood

'lance'). He was ultimately canonised and his body venerated in its own right at Mantua, although Notre-Dame-de-l'Isle at Lyon also claims to have his remains.

Various lances are claimed to be the actual spear used to pierce the side of Jesus. By the 11th century there was a lance at Antioch, another at Pharos, several in Constantinople, one in the Armenian church at Etchmiadzin and another in Paris. One lance kept in Vienna is particularly fascinating. It is known as the Spear of Destiny because it symbolises the realisation of the prophecies pointing to the Messiah. The earliest Christians, Jewish by birth, saw in the unwitting actions of the soldiers the fulfilment of Isaiah's prophecy that 'not a bone of him shall be broken' and Zechariah's prophecy that 'they will look on Him whom they have pierced'. Thus the lance played its part in the Messiah's destiny, and that of the whole human race.

Black with age, the relic consists of two parts joined together by a silver sheath. The top is long and tapers into a point, and the base has two metal flanges representing the wings of a dove. In the upper blade a hammer-headed nail is held fast by a cuff which is threaded with gold, silver and copper wire, and on the lowest sides of the base are embossed gold crosses.

THE SPEAR of Destiny is usually kept in an open leather case on a red velvet dais, in the Treasure House of the Hofburg in Vienna. It is on public view from Monday to Saturday (9am to 6pm).

ST HELENA

SET ON THE TOWN HALL IN COLCHESTER, ESSEX, is a statue of Helena, mother of one of the most powerful Roman Emperors and promoters of Christianity, Constantine the Great. Despite a complete lack of historical proof, Helena is still held by many to have been the daughter of Old King Cole, Prince of Colchester, or alternatively of a local innkeeper. In fact, all the evidence points to Helena having been born at Drepanum (Helenopolis), in Asia Minor, in about 255. Whatever the true facts may be, Helena has become a legend in her own right, as the intrepid seeker and collector of holy Christian relics.

FAR MORE IS KNOWN ABOUT the men who played significant parts in Helena's life than about Helena herself. She was lifted from her relatively lowly rank – probably the daughter of an innkeeper in the Middle East – by the Emperor Constantius Chlorus, who made Helena his wife. Their eldest son, Constantine, was born in 274. Eighteen years later, Helena was rejected by Constantius, who was busily extending his political power: he became Caesar in 292, taking on the rule of the British Isles, Gaul and Spain, and was subsequently crowned Emperor Augustus of all the Western Territories in 305. In the following year, however, Constantius Chlorus died at York, and Helena's fortunes changed again. Their son Constantine was proclaimed emperor by the Roman army – to the displeasure of several rival parties, and insisted that his mother be treated with honour and respect.

By 308 there were no fewer than six Roman emperors: Constantine, Maximian and Maxentius in the west; Galerius, Licinius and Maximilian in the east. Constantine had to survive several conflicts before his last great victory in 312, at the Mihian Bridge, against Maxentius' army. It was before this decisive battle that Constantine had a vision of a flaming cross inscribed with the words 'By this conquer'. From then on he and his mother were active in spreading the Christian faith. Helena was, in fact, one of the first of Constantine's followers to be baptised. Toleration and civic rights were extended to Christians under the Edict of Milan in 313 and, as Constantine increased his power base, the sphere of Christian influence was enlarged.

By 314 the Empire was again divided into east, ruled by Lucinius, and west, ruled by Constantine. A war between the two led to the cession of Illyricum, Pannonia and Greece to Constantine and a further victory in 324 gave him sole control of the Roman world. He made his capital in Byzantium, changing its name to Constantinople, or 'City of Constantine'.

Helena's travels

In 326 Helena, now in her 70s, set off on her travels to Jerusalem, determined to seek out the cross on which Jesus had died. It may well have been a wise move on her part: in the same year, Constantine executed his own son, Crispus, for treason, and his second wife, Fausta, met the same fate in the following year.

On her long visit to the Holy Land, Helena spent

large sums of money on relief projects and on the foundation of churches on traditional sacred sites. Her main goal, however, remained the discovery of the True Cross. Since the end of the 4th century Helena has been associated with the unearthing of a cross near Mount Calvary – although early accounts made no mention of her, and she may even have died before the actual discovery.

According to tradition, Helena ordered the destruction of Hadrian's 100m terrace, built over the hill and topped with a statue of Jupiter and a temple dedicated to Venus. Helena is said to have been shown the relevant spot in a dream and ordered labourers to dig there. Three crosses were then unearthed. Some sources relate how Helena conducted an experiment to discover which of the three had borne the body of Christ by directing a sick man to each cross in turn and praying for the True Cross to aid his recovery. After lying on two crosses with no effect, the invalid was cured as soon as he touched the third, which was proclaimed to be the Cross of the Saviour.

A church was built on the site, apparently under Helena's instructions, and the intrepid woman took a piece of the wood and two nails (which had been found near by) back home, where they were enshrined in a new church, the Holy Cross in Jerusalem (see page 36).

Helena died at Nicomedia in about 330, seven years before Constantine. Her feast day is celebrated every year on 18 August, and the Church keeps the feast of the Finding of the Cross by St Helena on 3 May.

LEFT: St Helena taking the Holy Cross to Jerusalem
CENTRE: St Helena, by Holbein

OPPOSITE PAGE: St Helena discovers the True Cross

THE SHROUD
OF TURIN

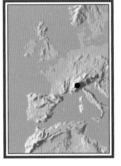

AFTER THE DEATH of Jesus, Joseph of Arimathea asked Pilate for the body, which he wrapped in linen cloths with a mixture of myrrh and aloes, and laid in his own tomb, newly hewn. When Peter and John ran to the empty tomb on Easter morning, they found the discarded burial cloths lying on the ground.

It was understandable that the original cloths would be kept and treasured, but over the centuries there was the inevitable proliferation of shrouds. By the end of the Crusades a hundred or more burial cloths purporting to be genuine had been brought back from the Holy Land and distributed all over Europe. By the middle of the 19th century there were still 42 claiming authenticity, and the most famous of these was the shroud kept in the cathedral at Turin, given to Ludovico of Savoy in the 15th century.

This long, narrow strip of linen, just over a metre wide and about 4m in length, displayed a series of curious brownish stains which, seen from a distance, revealed two life-size outlines of a man – one of the front of his body, the other of his back – lying head to head.

Positively Jesus?

In 1898 the Shroud of Turin was photographed for the first time. To everyone's astonishment, the large negative revealed an extraordinary detailed positive image of a man who had been scourged and crucified – the image on the cloth itself was, in effect, like a photographic negative, reversing the values of light and dark.

This unexpected discovery set in motion a series of eager investigations. More photographs

BELOW: a full-length view of the Turin Shroud

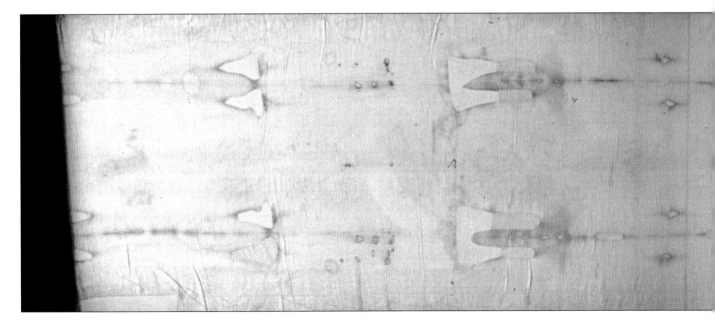

were produced, archives were carefully searched for any documentary corroboration, and biblical scholars found the shroud to be in 'complete harmony' with the gospel narrative. Pope Pius XI (1922–39) said that he 'was convinced of its authenticity', and Pius XII (1939–58) 'commended the universal veneration of this great relic of the Passion of Our Divine Saviour'. Millions of pilgrims surged into Turin for a series of public displays.

As confidence developed, experts from around the world were allowed access to the shroud. Scientists examined the cloth itself, using infra-red photography, X-rays, radiography and microscopic analysis (detecting traces of ancient pollen and spores found in the Holy Land). Art experts declared that no artist could have painted it (it would have required an understanding of negative imagery which only came about with the invention of photography), neither were there any traces of pigment. Doctors pointed out that the anatomical details were perfect, and pathologists agreed that crucifixion was almost certainly the cause of death.

Others hypothesised that the shroud's history included an early period of veneration in the Eastern church. Folded to show only the face, it could have been the model for icons and paintings of Jesus, accounting for the similarity of ancient depictions of Christ, especially the large, staring eyes (actually the closed lids of the corpse).

Sceptics in pursuit

In spite of the mountain of evidence, sceptics persisted in requesting yet more tests, some of which were unacceptable because they would have destroyed too much of the shroud. Then, in 1988, an American microchemist and investigator of frauds, Dr Walter McCrone, examined samples taken from the cloth. When he found traces of iron oxide, a pigment much used in the Middle Ages, believers could accept that the original faded image may have been enhanced. But the results of subsequent carbondating pleased the sceptics, as the cloth seemingly dated back only to the 13th century.

Nevertheless, believers in the authenticity of the shroud remain undeterred. They have more faith in the shroud than in the accuracy of scientific measurement, and point out that no scientist has ever satisfactorily explained how the image was imprinted on the cloth. Held in a silver reliquary, which is kept in an iron box inside an urn on the altar of Turin cathedral's Cappella della Sacra Sindone, it holds a universal fascination. (The chapel was designed by Guarino Guarini in the 17th century to house the shroud.) Only on special occasions is the shroud put on public view.

Is this the face of Christ?

ALTHOUGH THE SHROUD OF TURIN is hidden away, a photographic image is exhibited in the cathedral. This reveals the gaunt and bearded face of a man wearing a crown of thorns, and a body bearing wounds and bruises which are compatible with the effects of whip lashes, carrying a heavy object and being stabbed in the side with a spear.

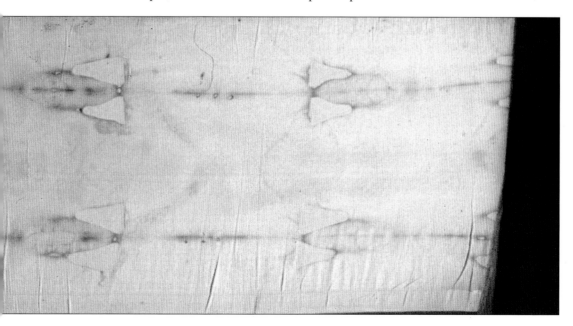

LORETO

Among the many Holy Houses in existence during the Middle Ages, the most famous was enshrined in the basilica at Loreto, near Ancona in Italy. This plain, rectangular room is claimed to be the place where Jesus grew up.

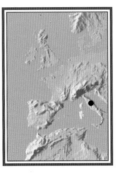

AFTER THE ASSUMPTION of Mary into heaven, her simple brick-built dwelling, only 9m long and 4m wide, which is now displayed at Loreto, is said to have been used as a church by the Apostles.

Years later, when the Romans looted and ravaged the Holy Land in AD 70 as punishment for the Jewish Revolt, they were apparently prevented by heavenly agencies from touching or entering the Holy House, which was thus miraculously preserved. St Helena, the mother of Constantine the Great, on her tireless search for relics in the 4th century (see pages 38–9), saw to it that a basilica was built over the House.

BELOW: Loreto, home of the most celebrated Holy House in Europe

In 1291, it is said, when the Holy Land had been sacked and conquered by the Saracens, four angels descended from Heaven and took possession of the Holy House in order to protect it from the sacrilegious hands of the 'invaders'. Then they transplanted it from Nazareth to a new, hilltop location between Fiume and Tersatto on the Dalmatian coast.

The Dalmatians gave the Holy House a friendly welcome, and for three years and seven months it was kept there as a holy shrine, visited by many pilgrims. Then, for no very apparent reason, the angels came again by night, took up the building and moved it to a temporary site in a wood near Recanati.

Only a few months later they returned and moved it yet again, this time to its present site: in a grove of laurel on a hill in the town of Loreto.

Loreto today

Loreto, whose name derives from the Latin *laurentum* (laurel), has been one of the most popular shrines of the Blessed Virgin Mary in Europe, visited by over 50 popes, and is the final destination of a pilgrimage undertaken by millions of people every year, particularly at Easter and at the Feast of the Holy House in December.

The landscape surrounding Loreto is not as immediately impressive as the Pyrenees, which almost encircle Lourdes, but there is fine scenery here, nevertheless, with distant mountains, pine woods, drifts of wild flowers and all the rural attractions of small farming country. Quiet, small towns packed with magnificent art and architecture punctuate the mountain valleys, just waiting to be discovered.

Loreto is situated south of Ancona, a port on the Adriatic coast, and is easily reached by local train (less easily by road). From the railway station a flight of steps leads up the hill to a Polish war cemetery, where a thousand or so men are buried, killed in various battles fought across this part of Italy during World War II. Further up the hill, dominating the town, is the Basilica of the Holy House, designed by some of the great Italian architects, such as Bramante and Sansovino: in the foreground is a large piazza with a central fountain, set against the basilica's overwhelming white frontage, bronze doors, bell-tower and statue of Pope Sixtus V (1585–90). The impressive 16th-century Palazzo Apostolico now functions as a museum and a hostel for sick or infirm pilgrims.

Inside there are many of the usual sights and sounds of liturgy: the candles and the votive lamps, the strong smell of incense, the colourful stained glass and swirling frescos, a gold-crowned and gem-encrusted icon of the Madonna and of course the Holy House (Santa Casa) itself.

Relics of Mary

ALTHOUGH TWO-THIRDS of the 6,000 shrines now attended in Europe are devoted to the Virgin Mary, these are of predominantly spiritual or mystical significance, as few relics are associated with Mary – but there are several, nevertheless.

Mary's tunic and many other items of her clothing were claimed to have been discovered in Galilee during the 4th century, and these and her shroud were soon being revered in Constantinople.

By the 6th century there was a collection of Mary's girdles, one of which, woven of camel's hair, is still held at the monastery of Vatopedi on Mount Athos, where the Greek Orthodox monks also possess the gifts of the Magi which she is said to have preserved.

A feather which was reported to have fallen from one of the wings of the angel Gabriel at the Annunciation is kept in Spain; another version of the legend claims that Gabriel gave Mary the feather to show Joseph that she had experienced a heavenly visitation.

Charlemagne had one of Mary's veils, as well as a lock of her hair, now found in Rheims Cathedral.

The Virgin Mary is supposed to have been suckling the infant Jesus in a cave when some of her precious milk fell on the stones and turned them brilliant white.

Several caves between Bethlehem and Nazareth are claimed as the site, the most popular being the Milk Grotto in the Church of the Nativity (see pages 16–18). By the 7th century the limestone and chalk dust from these caves was being collected by pilgrims and soon, mixed with water, was being offered for consumption as Mary's milk, 'a remedy for all womanly ills'.

Crystal phials of Mary's milk could be found in sanctuaries all over Europe, and the pilgrim's route to Walsingham, in East Anglia (see pages 115–17), was called the Milky Way because of the drops of 'Our Lady's Holy Milk' on display for veneration in the Holy House.

A relief at the Milk Grotto

Vatopedi Monastery in Greece, founded in the late 10th century

RIGHT: *the Basilica of the Holy House in Loreto*

BELOW: *Sansovino's Annunciation is one of the reliefs decorating the outer walls of the Holy House*

The outer walls of the building are elaborately clad in marble, and one has a screen carved to designs by Bramante, a contemporary of Michelangelo: *Sibyls and Prophets and the Life of the Virgin.* It comes as a welcome contrast to see the relative simplicity of the interior, where the walls have retained their original brickwork, although one end of the house has been equipped with an altar, and the wall behind it contains yet more marble and bronze decoration.

THERE ARE ANCIENT DOCUMENTS which state that the Holy House was taken from Nazareth to Loreto after the Crusades by a Byzantine family of imperial origin named Degli Angeli. Medals sold at Loreto show the Holy House being transported on board a ship.

VISIONS OF MARY

MOST SHRINES to the Virgin Mary are shrines without relics, though several of those marking the sites of visions have statues which are said to have shed tears or smiled, or which have been crowned with flowers that never died, and so on. Tales of such phenomena have been common enough since the Middle Ages, and stories still appear in newspapers to this day. Some have been proved hoaxes, others remain unexplained.

Many people have had visions of the Virgin Mary, often in the context of consecrated solitude: the deserts of the church fathers, the cells of the hermits and the cloisters of the monks were frequently comforted with night visions in which Mary reassured the devout of the heavenly rewards to come.

Several male Roman Catholic saints have left accounts of seeing and hearing Mary, and of talking with her like a child with a loving mother. The language in which these visions have been described is often beautiful, glowing with tenderness, sometimes passionate, occasionally even erotic, but such visions rarely, if ever, result in pilgrimage to the sites where they occurred. This may be because they are granted for personal reasons of psychological or spiritual necessity, rather than for the institution of public causes close to the heart of Mary or her Church.

Similar phenomena have been shared by mature women in the religious life, such as St Catherine of Siena or St Theresa of Lisieux.

Their visions tend to be coloured by profound yearnings for mystical union with their Lord Jesus; visions of Mary are far less frequent or intense, and mostly about her mothering of the divine child. But, again, apart from the institution of the Holy Medal (see page 46), there are relatively few exterior results – though the inner life is always enriched.

Most recent visions of Mary have been experienced by children, and especially by semi-literate teenage girls living in poverty-stricken farming communities.

LEFT: St Catherine of Siena, a 14th-century Dominican nun who was a mediator during the wars between Florence and the Pope, and whose visions and raptures attracted a wide following

The Holy Medal

There have been an extraordinary number of visions of Mary over the past 170 years or so. For example, during the 1830s, Catherine Laboure, while still a novice in the Daughters of Charity at their Mother House in Paris, received 'the most remarkable visionary favours from the Mother of God', and was entrusted with spreading throughout the world a new prayer and a new Holy Medal in honour of the Virgin.

IN 1980 A PLASTER STATUE of the Madonna wept tears of blood in a village not far from Milan. A war invalid was allowed to sip some, and was later able to throw away his walking stick. Then the owner of the statue was caught squirting pinkish water with his son's water pistol at the face of the statue. He admitted the deception, but could not tell the authorities why he had done it.

ABOVE: the Holy Medal, made to the Virgin Mary's own instructions

Catherine had all the makings of a saint. From an early age she had fasted on Fridays and Saturdays, and at the age of 23, despite parental opposition, she started her postulation at the House of Charity. Within a few nights she had a vision of the Blessed Virgin in the deserted chapel: a lady of great beauty who seated herself in the sanctuary, and on whose lap Catherine confidently rested her hands in prayer.

Their first conversation lasted two hours, during which time the Blessed Virgin told her that the times were evil, that the whole world would be afflicted by misery of every kind, that the cross would be despised and that blood would flow in the streets – and at this, the eyes of the Virgin filled with tears of compassion.

Four months later, the Blessed Virgin, bathed in light, again showed herself to Catherine as she knelt in the chapel, this time with her sisters. Nobody else could see the vision, but Catherine was enraptured, and was given the design and instructions for the making of a Holy Medal, an oval-shaped medallion, which would bear the image of the Virgin as the Immaculate Conception on one face of it, with a mystical monogram on the other.

She was also given a prayer 'straight from the Courts of Heaven to earth': 'O Mary, conceived without sin, pray for us who have recourse to Thee'.

The diffusion of this medal and its prayer was accompanied by innumerable miraculous cures and startling conversions, and after her death Catherine was canonised.

There is no special pilgrimage associated with Catherine's visions, though the Daughters of Charity at the rue du Bac in Paris allow visitors to venerate her preserved body in its glass-fronted case under the altar in the chapel, where Our Lady appeared to her.

Many other visions of Mary have been claimed since, most of which have failed to catch the imagination of the faithful. Regardless of popular response, however, such visions are always stringently investigated by the Church authorities. Some are approved after serious consideration, some are condemned as false, while in other cases a wait-and-see attitude is deemed appropriate.

RIGHT: one of the many phenomena associated with the Virgin Mary: a statue that is said to weep tears of blood in Medugorje (see pages 61–2)

Real or imagined?

Precisely why any of these visions is taken more seriously than any other is a puzzling question to non-believers, but in the case of spurious visions, interest soon dies out. For example, there was a case quite recently, south-west of Lyon in France, where a 14-year-old girl claimed no fewer than 31 visions of the Virgin Mary. People flocked there on foot, by car, bicycle, coach and train – not just from the four corners of France, but from as far afield as Italy, Germany and Switzerland.

The visions mostly took place in a vegetable garden behind the tumbledown cottage where the girl lived with her parents and brothers and sisters, though on at least one occasion it happened while she was sitting at a table in the kitchen. She described the lady as appearing in a shining white light, and being tall, young, and dressed in a long blue dress and white veil. The lady apparently told her that she wanted a basilica built there, and said that she much preferred Mass to be celebrated in Latin.

Presented with this account, the local priest said that the girl was simply a dreamer who should not be encouraged to look at so many pictures of the saints. Yet, on the surface the details were not unlike those cases discerned to be authentic: a lone, pious adolescent girl, an unlikely place for visions and priestly condescension (even the bulk purchase of statuettes of the Virgin by locals hoping for a profit). In due course, however, interest faded away.

This particular site was not to reach the stage of international acclaim enjoyed by some other places of pilgrimage. Perhaps the most famous example of celebrated sites, where public attention has been sustained and increased, is the shrine at Lourdes.

ABOVE: eager crowds wait for another manifestation of the Madonna

BELOW: the relics of visionary St Theresa are paraded through Lisieux. This 19th-century Carmelite nun died of tuberculosis at the age of 24 after writing her hugely popular memoirs, published posthumously

LOURDES

In the mid-19th century the experiences of an unassuming teenage girl brought Lourdes to the attention of the world. On the bank of the River Gave the Virgin Mary appeared to Bernadette Soubirous, and a quiet rural spot began its transformation into a centre of pilgrimage.

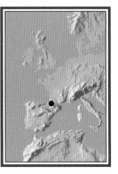

OPPOSITE PAGE: the Supérieure (1871) is one of three basilicas in Lourdes. The church of Rosaire was built in 1889 and St-Pie X, the world's biggest underground basilica, was built in 1958 to house 20,000 worshippers

MOST PILGRIMS heading for the healing waters of the shrine of the Blessed Virgin at Lourdes travel there by train. From Paris it is a beautiful journey to the south through the ancient and historic cities of Orléans, Tours and Poitiers, to the port of Bordeaux, and then gradually eastwards through the dark pine forests to trace the course of the River Gave de Pau up into the foothills of the High Pyrenees, along the curve of the valley between the river and the tumbled rocks, the pine trees and the towering peaks and eventually to Lourdes.

Mountains encircle the town where, beyond the river, there rises the great rock of Massabielle. At its foot is the grotto of the Blessed Virgin, flanked and guarded by many hundreds of candles, all burning constantly,

A personal account of Lourdes

A GIRL OF 18 OR 19 approaches the grotto on her knees, a slow metre or so at a time, her stockings rolled down to her ankles, both knees grazed and bleeding from the small sharp stones.

A PRIEST DRINKS the healing water to wash down three small white tablets, quickly and discreetly.

A DEAF MAN and wife pray in sign language, in rapt devotion and silence.

A MAN LEANS against the rocks by the entrance, racked by sobs. Every so often he regains control, dries his eyes, and starts his rosary once more, gazing up at the Virgin in hope and trust – but then his emotion gets the better of him, and he buries his face in his hands. Another man goes over to him, puts his arm around the heaving shoulders, comforts him and prays with him.

A MOTHER holds up her baby towards the Mother of Mothers, arms rigid. The mother is blind, her baby disabled.

A BOY AND A GIRL in their early 20s, finishing their prayers, help each other up from their knees, and kiss shyly. Both are disabled; the girl has a shrivelled left arm.

NUNS LOOK UP at the Virgin while they photograph each other in the posture of prayer.

AN OLD MAN and his wife sit side by side, holding hands like young lovers, saying their rosary with one set of beads, taking turns to recite the Hail Mary. Both are in wheelchairs; both have stunted legs.

A MOTHER pushes her adult son on a wheeled stretcher; he is paralysed from the shoulders down, deaf and with the mental age of a child. 'Taken me eight years to save the money to bring him,' she says. 'It's the only hope there is, to have Our Lady smiling down in mercy upon him. Our Lady was a mother herself, so she must know what it's like, mustn't she? I mean, she can't refuse eight years of sacrifice, can she?' She joins the queues with hundreds of others. There are no miracles of healing to be seen among them – only miracles of faith.

ABOVE: the visionary, Bernadette Soubirous

night and day, like a galaxy of distant stars. Soaring above the rock is the slender spire of a white marble church. This is Lourdes, the largest and most famous centre of pilgrimage in the Roman Catholic world, which draws millions of people to its underground spring every year in search of spiritual healing or a miraculous cure.

The history

In 1858 a 14-year-old local peasant girl, Marie Bernarde 'Bernadette' Soubirous, claimed that the Blessed Virgin Mary had appeared to her as a 'lady all in white', at the entrance to a small cave in the great rock of Massabielle, and that a spring of water had bubbled up from the earth.

Bernadette was the eldest daughter of an impoverished miller's labourer, a 'shiftless liar' who had been imprisoned for theft a year before the first of his daughter's visions. Her mother had a quick temper: her main method of child-rear-

DURING 1958, the centenary of St Bernadette's visions, 6 million pilgrims made their way to the grotto at Lourdes.

ing was the use of what Bernadette called 'the dreaded cudgel' in a 'good beating'.

Both parents were drunkards, the family was destitute, and all of their unfortunate children were most shamefully neglected. Bernadette, in the words of her contemporaries, was 'weak and feeble at her birth', and 'always ailing and sickly'. At the age of five or six 'asthma seized her in its iron grip ... fits of coughing took her, she would be almost suffocated and fall into prolonged swoons'. (JB Estrade, *The Appearances of the Blessed Virgin at the Grotto of Lourdes*, Clonmore and Reynolds Ltd, 1946.) She remained a chronic asthmatic all through her short life.

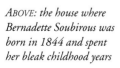

ABOVE: the house where Bernadette Soubirous was born in 1844 and spent her bleak childhood years

In the opinion of the woman who tried to teach her to read even the simplest words and sentences, 'she would never be anything but an ignorant fool'. According to another account, at the age of 14, when she had the visions of Mary, she was a 'stunted girl, both physically and mentally retarded, starved of both love and attention, tormented by delayed growth into womanhood'.

On 2 February 1858 Bernadette went with her younger sister and another small girl to the dump to search for firewood and perhaps find bones and old iron to sell to the local scrap merchant. This dump was at the bend of the River Gave where people threw their domestic rubbish and sewage. She was about to wade across the shallow river when, in her own words, she 'heard a noise ... I raised my head and looked at the cave, and saw a lady dressed all in white. She was wearing a white dress and a blue sash and a yellow rose on each foot the colour of the chain of her rosary.' The vision disappeared suddenly, but was to be only the first in a sequence of 18 altogether, which continued on and off until the middle of the following July.

At the end of the series of visions their fame had spread far and wide, and thousands of people would assemble and wait for hours to watch the little girl kneeling entranced in the mud – even though nobody else ever saw or heard anything, and nobody else ever knew what the lady was supposed to have said to her in any detail. The lady has never returned there since.

There is no reason to doubt the sincerity of Bernadette. She had very little to gain by deliberate deceit or pretence. As a result of her claims to have seen and talked with 'her lady' she was subjected to vicious and brutal beatings from her mother, accusations of fraud, suspicions of mental derangement and even madness, repeated ordeals of police interrogation, and hours and hours of relentless and unsympathetic examination by priests and bishops – all of which she bore with patience and fortitude.

The experience and its aftermath did, eventually, allow Bernadette to live out the few remaining years of her life in the comparative comfort of the convent of the Daughters of Charity at Nevers, where she died at the age of 35. This simple, self-effacing woman could not have forseen her ultimate canonisation in 1933.

The first miracle at Lourdes was that of a quarryman who had lost the sight of one eye in an accident at work, and claimed it was immediately and completely restored after rinsing his face in the water. There was soon a trickle of other miracles, then a steady flow, and then a flood. Hundreds and thousands of cures were announced for every disease under the sun, until tens of thousands of people were surging every year through the valley and the growing town in search of health and healing.

As the claims grew wilder and increasingly more exaggerated, sceptics began to ask awkward questions and even sincere believers became embarrassed. Finally, the Roman Catholic Church called a halt. A medical bureau was established in Lourdes to investigate all reported cures and healings and, not surprisingly, the flood faltered, slowed down, and very soon ceased to be so much as a trickle. From the heady statistics of three or four thousand a year, only 98 cures were accepted as even remarkable between 1925 and 1950, of which a mere 11 were pronounced as 'genuine miracles'.

LEFT: The Chapel of St Bernadette in the church of Rosaire

Nevertheless, the Church has approved some accounts, and thousands of people, often with incurable diseases, still make the costly trip to Lourdes in the desperate hope of remedy and recovery.

Lourdes today

The first experience of any pilgrimage to Lourdes is the dominant sound of the bells in the church above the rock of Massabielle, ringing the almost endlessly repetitive tune of the *Hymn to Our Lady* and playing successive notes to mark every quarter-of-an-hour:

LEFT: prayers are offered to the Virgin Mary as new pilgrims light new candles

RIGHT: medallions, statuettes and other souvenirs are big business in most major sites of pilgrimage

ABOVE: the fountain of water said to cure all ills, in the grotto where Mary first appeared to Bernadette

BELOW: invalids wait in their wheelchairs to sample the waters of Lourdes

O Benigna! on the first quarter; *O Benigna! O Regina!* on the second quarter; *O Benigna! O Regina! O Maria!* on the third, and then, on the hour, every hour, the complete invocation: *Ave! Ave! Ave Maria! Ave! Ave! Ave Maria!*

Day and night, night and day, day after day, the song is ever present, ringing out above all the other sounds of Lourdes: the urgent waters of the River Gave splashing and tumbling among the rocks, the loudspeakers booming across the town from the Masses and Benedictions and processions to and from the grotto.

The pilgrims sing the hymn over and over again, their feet walk it, they live and breathe and pray and sleep it; and always and everywhere, the bells of the church go on sounding it: *Ave! Ave! Ave Maria! Ave! Ave! Ave Maria!*

Two splendid basilicas were built beside the original grotto, and a third underground basilica, dedicated to Pope Pius X and capable of accommodating 20,000 pilgrims, was opened in 1958, to commemorate the centenary of the visions.

The grotto itself is an extremely peaceful acre of holy ground. There is certainly more simple piety expressed there than at any other Christian shrine in the world, so that even visitors who are not true believers are genuinely impressed and often genuinely moved. The river flows near by, cows graze in the meadow, birds swoop and flutter and sing through the trees, and the ranks of candles burn, in all sizes from the thickness of a finger to the full height of a man, flickering and guttering, pale by day and bright by night. The rocks above the grotto are now blackened with generations of this candle smoke, and the air is always pungent with the smell of hot and sizzling wax. Next to the grotto is the fountain where people come to drink and bathe in the waters.

Hundreds and thousands of people, men and women, young and old, come to pray at this spot, quietly, lovingly, reverently, looking up trustingly at the statue of Our Lady of Lourdes set in the niche where she appeared to Bernadette.

They kneel before her, imploring, beseeching, weeping with their private pain or smiling with inner joy; sometimes they leave little gifts and messages for her; they prostrate themselves before her, saying the rosary with the beads in their laps or with their arms stretched out to her; or they merely sit there, lost in meditation and devotion, gazing up into the face of the Queen of Heaven.

FATIMA

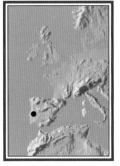

FATIMA IS A VILLAGE in Portugal, about 150km north of Lisbon, in a largely arid mountain region which produces a little dry wine, a little olive oil, figs, fruit and vegetables. The hard work of peasants also forces this ungrateful soil to yield harvests of wheat and maize. The language spoken there is the *lingua rustica* of ancient Lusitania, basically the Latin of the Roman Empire, a reminder of an earlier occupation.

Here, in 1917, a lady 'made entirely of light' appeared on six occasions to three children: Lucia de Jesus Santos, Francisco Marto and his little sister Jacinta.

The history

It was Sunday, 13 May 1917, towards the end of the 'war to end all wars'. After early morning Mass, the three little shepherds were watching their flocks in the Cova da Iria, a shallow depression of arid land, not far from their home. Lucia, aged 10, was reserved and had always wanted to be a saint. Francisco, aged nine, was a lively boy who liked to hunt snakes and lizards. Jacinta, his sister, the 'Little Flower of the Mountains', was an affectionate child with a sweet voice.

At noon there was a vivid flash of lightning. The children thought there was going to be a storm, and decided to gather the sheep to safety, but there was another dazzling flash, and they were enveloped in a blinding light. They saw a lady 'brighter than the sun', her 'bare and rosy feet resting on an ermine cloud' which just touched the branches of a rather stunted holm-oak. They immediately fell into an ecstasy, and contemplated her. The three were to report differing experiences of the vision. Lucia saw and heard the lady, clearly and distinctly, and conversed with her; Francisco only saw her, and heard nothing; and Jacinta saw clearly, but heard less distinctly. They described the vision as lovelier than any person they had ever met: young, about 18 at the most, dressed simply in white with a golden cord fastening her dress around her neck. A mantle of white with edges decorated by a delicate thread of gold covered her head and shoulders, and draped gracefully down almost to the hem of her dress. Her face, pure and exquisitely fine-featured, was smiling with a touch of sadness, and her hands were joined in prayer. From her right arm there hung a rosary, the beads of pearly whiteness, the cross of burnished silver. With a maternal gesture, she spoke to the three children: 'Do not be afraid, I will do you no harm.'

'Where do you come from, my lady?' asked Lucia.

'I come from Heaven.'

'What do you want of me?' said Lucia.

The lady said she wanted them to 'come here for the next six months, on the 13th day of each month, at this hour', and asked: 'Will you offer yourselves to God and accept all the sufferings he will send you in reparation for the numberless sins which offend his divine majesty? Will you suffer to obtain the conversion of sinners?'

'Yes,' said Lucia eagerly, speaking for all three, 'we will'.

The lady signified her pleasure at this answer. Their conversation continued for about 10 minutes, during which time Jacinta

ABOVE: *the first vision of Lady Mary experienced by three local children is re-created in the Fatima Museum of Waxworks*

RIGHT: a church procession
passes among the tourists
and pilgrims in Fátima

ABOVE: a pilgrim at prayer,
alone among the crowds

suggested giving the lady some of their lunch of bread and cheese, and then the lady departed in an intense ray of light and vanished in the radiant light of the sun.

Lucia's mother accused her of lying, and thrashed her with a broomstick so that, as one of her sisters observed, 'not even St Anthony could have taken away her bruises'. Most other people were unimpressed with the children's story, and life went on as usual.

But because the lady had asked them to 'suffer to obtain the conversion of sinners', the children began fasting every day, giving their lunch of bread and cheese to their sheep or to local beggars. They would prostrate themselves on the rocky ground and pray for hours, and, as one priest wrote, 'they developed a thirst for suffering' by beating their own naked legs with nettles and wearing 'penitential girdles' of hard rope around the waist under their clothes.

A month later, at the promised time and place, there was another vision: a 10-minute conversation during which the lady revealed the early deaths of Francisco and Jacinta and urged 'devotion to the Immaculate Heart of Mary'. As she departed, there was a loud noise like a rocket exploding, and the 40 or 50 people who had been present, though they saw or heard nothing of the lady, saw a white cloud rising and moving towards the east.

Lucia received another severe thrashing as a wicked liar, while the parish priest said it might even be the work of the devil.

The third vision, in July, attracted 4,000 people, all waiting to see or hear something. There was more blazing light and another conversation, during which the lady imparted a secret message to Lucia, and all three of them were vouchsafed a glimpse of Hell: 'A great sea of fire, black and burning demons and hideous beasts, souls in human form resembling live translucent coals, loud screams and cries of pain and despair.'

Lucia's mother remained incredulous, and once again gave the child a sound thrashing with the broomstick. There was continued opposition from the priest and many of the villagers, and the three children were actually abducted by the civic authorities to prevent them from being present at the promised time and place of the fourth vision. However 18,000 people assembled, heard a tremendous clap of thunder, watched the beautiful, misty cloud, saw it slowly move away to the east and were enraptured. So it went on, and even Lucia's mother relented, though she retained her doubts.

An estimated 30,000 assembled for the fifth vision on 13 September. A globe of light ascended majestically across the sky, and a shower of mysterious white flakes, or rose

petals, descended from the sun. The children were warned by the lady that her next appearance would be her last, and that it would be marked by a great miracle, and she enjoined them to recite the rosary every day.

In Lisbon the Roman Catholic press continued a solemn reserve, and warned its readers to 'beware the possible machinations of the Powers of Darkness'.

The last vision

In Fátima, on the morning of 13 October, the children had been dressed in their best, with the little girls in blue dresses with white mantles and embroidered flowers on their veils, holding posies in their hands and wearing crowns of roses on their heads.

The crowd at the sixth and final vision was estimated at anything from 70,000 to 100,000, and events went on much as they had before; except that this time it was pouring with rain, cold and dismal, and the place had become a quagmire. The rain suddenly ceased, and the onlookers could see a white cloud rising around and above the children, though none of the witnesses heard anything. Those who could see Lucia reported that she fell into an immediate ecstasy, her face becoming more and more beautiful as it was flushed with a rosy tint.

'Lady', said Lucia, 'who are you, and what do you want of me?'

'I am Our Lady of the Rosary. I want a chapel built here in my honour. Continue to say the rosary every day.'

Then, as the conversation went on, she emphasised the need for 'an amendment in men's lives', because 'God was already too much offended'.

There were then various other visions to the right and left of the sun: St Joseph, the infant Jesus blessing the world, Mary herself as Our Lady of Sorrows, then Jesus, fully grown, again blessing the world, and, finally, Mary as Our Lady of Mount Carmel.

Then the onlookers saw the sun tremble; it appeared to hesitate in its course and, quite suddenly, began to whirl or rotate, throwing off great rays of the most fantastic colours in all directions: yellow, green, red, blue and violet, in a fearsome dance. The whole landscape turned purple, and then the sun, 'radiating a red radiance', seemed to fall and fall until it reached almost to the heads of the terrified onlookers, some of whom thought that the world was ending and claimed to have felt its intense heat. But then it stopped and slowly made its way back to its place in the firmament.

The whole event took only 12 minutes, just after noon at Fátima, and was witnessed

ABOVE: thousands of candles light the way as Our Lady is carried through the streets

BELOW: an artist's impression of the vision of Fátima, depicted on a Spanish card of 1950

ABOVE: up to 100,000 worshippers gather on the annual pilgrimage days in May and October to celebrate open-air Mass

BELOW: light at the end of the pilgrimage
OPPOSITE PAGE: a statue of Christ towers over Fátima before the white basilica, Portugal's largest church

by up to 100,000 people. There were a number of miraculous cures reported in the days that followed.

Two years later, at the age of 11, Francisco died of the Spanish influenza then ravaging Europe. To one Jesuit commentator the 'spiritualisation of this exquisite death' was 'almost proof positive of the authenticity of the visions'. Then a spring of clear fresh water bubbled up in that arid hollow where Our Lady had appeared to the children, and was taken as yet further proof.

Jacinta died of the same influenza at the age of only 10, just a year after her brother Francisco, her body 'exhaling a delicious perfume of flowers', and 'remaining incorrupt' even at the time of her reburial, 20 or so years afterwards.

THE SECRET OF Fátima, told by Our Lady to Lucia, is still talked about but has never yet been revealed to the waiting world. She confided it in writing to the Vatican in 1941 with the proviso it should not be announced before 1960. One legend relates that when Pope Pius XII read the secret he fainted; another is that the saintly Pope John XXIII (1958–63) read it, and decided that it should never be made public.

Lucia soon became a novice of the Dorothean Sisters and left Fátima, never to return. Eventually, desiring an even more contemplative life to meditate upon 'her great treasures', she joined the closed order of Carmelites at Coimbra.

Fátima today

The hollow of the Cova da Iria has been levelled and terraced, lined with avenues and planted with trees. At the far end of the vast arena rises the imposing Basilica of Our Lady of Fátima, the largest church in Portugal, a splendour of brilliant white stone with a graceful bell-tower surmounted by a large crown and cross. It boasts a magnificent flight of steps, 15 altars, a statue of Our Lady standing 4m high, white marble, colonnades and the little Chapel of the Visions (Capela das Aparições), built over the exact site of the apparitions. Inside are the tombs of the two children who died so young, Francisco and Jacinta Marto. It still attracts an almost incomprehensible number of pilgrims every year – estimated figures range between 100,000 and a couple of million.

ABOVE: as dusk falls the candles are lit, making midnight Mass a dramatic and moving spectacle

BELOW: even modern pilgrims need to be equipped to face the elements and the terrain on their long journey

A journey to Fátima can be one of the most memorable experiences a Christian pilgrim is ever likely to have – especially if it is made on any of the great feasts of the Blessed Virgin Mary: the Annunciation, or the Assumption, or, perhaps the most dramatic occasions of all, on 13 May or 13 October each year, the dates of the first and last vision, when there are torchlit processions, night vigils and Masses.

Pilgrims arrive on the previous afternoon and merge into the crowds pouring down the mountains into the valley, some in cars or coaches, some on bicycles, many on foot, having walked for days, some alone or in pairs, some in processions, most of them singing hymns of hope and affirmation. Most pilgrims, following the surge of the crowd, visit the little chapel built on the very spot where Our Lady of Fátima appeared. Here, they are witness to tears, joy and a depth of devotion rarely found except on High Days at Lourdes: believers rapt on their knees, the low murmur of the rosary being prayed in a bewildering number of languages, young

mothers holding their children up to touch the hem of Mother Mary's robe.

As it grows dark, here and there in that valley of reverence, hardly noticed in the dusk, there appear little glimmerings of light, floating on the slowly swirling sea of people: a few tentative candles at first, then dozens of candles, then hundreds, and soon thousands and tens of thousands, until eventually the sea is transmuted into fire.

At noon the next day, in the presence of this vast multitude, the statue of Our Lady of Fátima is carried in solemn procession from the little chapel to the high altar for the celebration of Mass, and she seems to float among the banners of her pilgrims. Suddenly, the air is filled with roses – showers of petals descending on her and her bearers and covering the ground at their feet.

Then, just as suddenly, the valley seems to be under snow, as thousands of handkerchiefs are waved and fluttered in salutation. Many people are by this time in tears – men, women, children and even the priests who have seen it all a hundred times before.

GARABANDAL

Set in the Santander province of northern Spain, San Sebastián de Garabandal is a village in remote and beautiful country, reached by a steep road, on foot. In this quiet place, in the early 1960s, yet more visions of Mary were claimed.

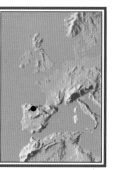

ON THE EVENING of 18 June 1961, four young girls were playing in a field just outside the village when they all heard a loud noise like thunder, and saw before them the bright figure of the Archangel Michael.

During the following days he appeared to them again in the same place, and announced that on the second day of July they would receive visions of Our Lady.

Conchita Gonzalez, Maria Dolores Mazon and Jacinta Gonzalez, all aged 12, and Maria Cruz Gonzalez, aged 11, came from poor families and were all semi-literate.

The news spread quickly. The appointed day, 2 July, was a Sunday, and the village was crowded with the curious. At six in the evening the girls went to the place where the archangel had appeared, and to the astonishment of the crowd they entered into ecstasy.

There, completely invisible to everybody else, and unheard, was the Lady. According to the children: 'She is dressed in a white robe with a blue mantle and a crown of golden stars. Her hands are slender. She carries the child Jesus in her arms. Her hair, deep nut-brown, is parted in the centre, and reaches down to her waist. Her face is long, with a fine nose. Her mouth is very pretty. She looks like a girl of 18. She is rather tall. There is no voice like hers, no woman so beautiful.' Our Lady had manifested herself again, and talked naturally with the girls like a mother to her daughters. After this there were more than 2,000 visions, several a week, over a period of five years. The girls did not always receive them together – sometimes only one would be favoured, at other times two or three – nor were they always at the same hour.

During the visions the girls went into ecstasies lasting from a few minutes to several hours. Time did not seem to matter, and they never showed any signs of being tired, despite their very often uncomfortable posture, kneeling on the rocks with their heads thrown violently backwards, or on the cold days of winter with snow under their bare feet. They lost all sense of pain, and powerful lights flashed into their eyes did not cause a flicker.

There were also ecstatic marches, when the girls would run forwards and backwards at high speed in the darkness of the night, without ever faltering, their bodies hardly subject to the laws of gravitation, but apparently endowed with spiritual agility.

There were thousands of witnesses; the children were subjected to hundreds of tests

AS ALWAYS, the Church has acted with caution and merely allowed that there is nothing to be condemned about the visions of Garabandal, although Conchita has been questioned by several cardinals, and has been received twice in private audience by the Pope.

BELOW: a plaque marks the place, at the base of a cedar tree, where Mary first appeared

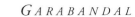

GARABANDAL

RIGHT: the remote village of Garabandal, where four young girls attracted the eyes of the world

by doctors and scientists, and investigated by television teams and reporters. Everyone involved with the phenomena agreed that what was happening to the girls seemed to have no obvious explanation.

The message

BELOW: a view of the village from the hilltop site of the apparitions

The message that had been passed on to the four chosen children was that they must 'do much penance and make many sacrifices. You must often visit the Blessed Sacrament. But above all you must be very good, for if you are not, you will be punished. The Chalice of Divine Wrath is already filling, and if you do not amend your lives there will come a Chastisement.'

The young Conchita eventually revealed the startling fact that she had been passed a 'secret message', the essence of which was that we could all expect a 'warning to come directly from God, the culmination of our sins to be seen and felt in all parts of the world and by every person'.

If the warning went unheeded, according to this revelation, there would be punishment. The chalice had been filling, and now it was flowing over into judgement. The Church, according to the message, was in a perilous state: 'Many cardinals, bishops, and priests are on the road to perdition, taking many souls with them.'

MEDUGORJE

Visions of the Madonna and child, and of Heaven and Hell, changed the face of a tiny Yugoslavian hamlet in the 1980s.

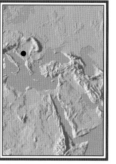

TWENTY YEARS AFTER the first vision appeared at Garabandal in Spain (see pages 59–60), more apparitions created another new pilgrimage site. They occurred in Međugorje, in what was then Yugoslavia, up in the mountains about an hour's drive from the Adriatic coast, among vines and terraces of tobacco.

The history

On Wednesday 24 June 1981, two girls who had been friends all their lives, Ivanka Ivankoric, aged 15, and Mirjana Dragicevic, aged 16, were walking up the hill behind the village. At around five o'clock, one of them saw a bright, shining figure of a young woman in the sky.

Later that evening, at dusk, with four other friends, they saw the Madonna with the baby Jesus in her arms, and on the following evening, just after six o'clock, they saw her yet again and talked with her for about five minutes. The news spread like wildfire, and thousands of people began to congregate for the vision on Friday, when a brilliant light shone over the village. By Sunday there were 15,000 people.

In vision after vision, the Serbo-Croat word for 'peace' appeared in huge, flame-coloured letters across 2 or 3km of night sky. A three-year-old boy who had been a deaf mute and virtually paralysed since birth was healed, reporters and television crews arrived in droves. The local parish priest remained unconvinced and dismissed the whole phenomenon as an example of mass hysteria.

What did the Madonna say to the girls? This was the reported version: 'I am come as the Queen of Peace. Pray, fast, recommit yourselves to God, and, above all, be peaceful, have peace within yourselves, peace in the world.' There were also visions of Heaven, Purgatory and Hell.

By 1985 an estimated 2 or 3 million people had made the pilgrimage to Međugorje, with an estimated 100,000 on the fourth anniversary of the vision.

There were now four or five regular visionaries: three girls and two boys, and the visions were a daily event – nearly 2,000 in all, each evening at around 6.45 and also, for two years, twice a week late at night up on the hill at the back of the village.

The visionaries, who go into a rigid ecstasy similar to that exhibited by the girls at San Sebastián de Garabandal, sometimes for two minutes, occasionally for an hour, have been tested by doctors and scientists, who

LEFT: the once-crowded church of Međugorje, all but deserted during the years of civil war

have concluded that it is all inexplicable. The Church has acted with caution, adopting a wait-and-see attitude.

The life of the village has changed profoundly, every aspect of its existence has been affected. According to one villager, 'We don't swear any more, we don't get drunk. How can we when the Madonna comes to us each day?' Another told journalist Gitta Sereny: 'It is simple: we now care, not just about ourselves and our neighbours, but about all of the parish, and all of the world.'

Hope and devotion

vision which had thrown the word *Mir* – peace – across the sky. The town of Međugorje has not been bombed, the people have remained at peace, and the UN has set up its headquarters there. However, the house of the bishop of Mostar, who remained hostile to the visions, was destroyed in the war and he has since left the region.

Since the complex and vicious civil war in the area, and the breakup of the former Yugoslavia into conflicting regions, with factions fighting factions for reasons that are often baffling to the rest of the world, Međugorje is obviously more difficult to reach than it was, but the pilgrims have continued to arrive, even during the war, though in fewer numbers.

Međugorje today

BELOW: pilgrims erect simple crosses and wait for a new vision from Heaven

The war in the former Yugoslavia broke out exactly 10 years to the day after the first

GUADALUPE

·

*In the 16th century the powerful Spanish Church was astounded by tales
of the vision granted to a penniless local Indian.*

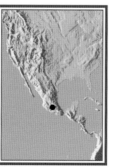

*I*T IS RARE TO find an example of Mary appearing to a grown man who is not a priest, or a monk, or a saint in the making, but an ordinary man with nothing except faith to recommend him. Yet such a vision gave birth to one of the most spectacular pilgrimages in existence: the pilgrimage to Guadalupe, north of downtown Mexico City.

The history

The story of Guadalupe had its beginnings among the impoverished Indians of Mexico, 10 years or so after the 16th-century Spanish conquest. The Aztec chiefs had been killed, many men and women and children sold into slavery, and all the tribal lands had been divided between the rapacious Conquistadores. After being liberated from the bondage of the Aztecs, whose religion demanded human sacrifice, the Mexican Indians found themselves under the covetous rule of the new Spanish colonists, who mined the precious metals and set up European-style agriculture, forming huge feudal estates. In both cases local Indians provided cheap labour.

But, as St Francis said, 'It is always the poor at their poorest to whom the greatest spiritual treasures are given.'

Early one Saturday morning, on 9 December 1531, one of the poorest of the poor, an illiterate Indian named Juan Diego was on his way past a barren hill sacred to the Aztec mother goddess, Tonantzin, in what is now Guadalupe.

Very little is known about Juan Diego, except that he was a widower in his late 50s, a convert whose original Indian name was Cuatitlatoatzin ('Eagle-who-talks').

In the words of a contemporary account (quoted in *The Marian Era*, Franciscan

J UAN DIEGO'S CLOAK has been examined by scientists, though not in quite the same depth as the Shroud of Turin. Photographic enlargement, microscopic and infra-red examination have been used, though there has been no need for carbon-dating as there is little doubt about its age or provenance. The Church authorities have long acknowledged what was evident to ordinary visual inspection: that the image has been over-painted several times, not always by skilled hands. Examination confirmed that the gold halo and the angel holding the moon were later additions. But there was an original image which had not been painted and which remained fresh and bright. There was also the face of La Indita: under high magnification her left eye appears to show the reflection of Juan Diego and the surprised bishop being presented with the cloak. How the original image was imprinted remains a mystery, though there is always the possibility that the ancient Aztecs had more secrets than we know about.

ABOVE: *several churches have been built in Guadalupe since Juan Diego's vision. The gold-domed cathedral dates from the late-19th century*

Herald Press, 1960), 'as he hurried along in the chill pre-dawn' the air was 'full of birdsong' and 'music of such clarity and sweetness that he stopped, entranced'. The barren rocks up there were 'clothed with a glowing cloud resplendent with many-coloured rays of light'.

Suddenly the singing faded, and Juan Diego heard a woman's voice calling softly to him from the cloud. He climbed the rocks in haste, and there was a 'young Indian maiden, clad in the garments of an Aztec Princess'. Ever afterwards he was to refer to her as 'La Indita', the Little Indian.

In his own words, which must have been somewhat embellished in the translation, 'Her robe shone so brightly that its glory trans-formed the rough rocks on the hilltop. The very stones appeared to be precious gems, and the leaves of the thorn bushes appeared to be clusters of fine emeralds, their twigs and stems like burnished gold.'

She called, and beckoned, and when he approached, she assured him in Náhuatl, his native tongue, that she was a 'loving mother to you and those like you' – which he took to mean the Indians – on the very hill held sacred by the Indians' former religion, which practised child sacrifice. The fact that she was wearing a special girdle reserved for pregnant women was a sign of her particular concern for children. She then went on to instruct him to go from there to the palace of the bishop, and inform

BELOW: *a colourful image of Our Lady of Guadalupe decorated with flowers*

him that she desired him to build her a church on the very place where she was standing.

Understandably, given the way the Spaniards usually treated Indians, poor Juan politely suggested that she send a Spaniard with such an important request. But she told him that she was acting from love for the downtrodden Indians, and promised that all would be well. So Juan Diego steeled himself for a flogging, at least, and went down the hill.

When he explained to the servants of the bishop that he had business with their master, they laughed at him and made him wait nearly all day. But, finally, moved by his patience, they let him in.

ABOVE: a mother carrying her baby makes the slow and painful approach to the cathedral on her knees

The bishop was dismissive of the very idea that Our Lady would appear to an Indian, and demanded a sign. Although dusk was falling by now, Juan went back up the hill, and La Indita made a garden of fragrant Castilian roses spring into abundance on the bare rocks. Under her directions, Juan gathered some, sparkling with dew, and carried them in his cloak back to the bishop. Upon opening his cloak it was seen that, miraculously, La Indita had imprinted her own vivid image on the inside of the coarse, homespun cloth.

The image is undoubtedly the most important symbol of Christianity in Mexico, because it shows a dark-skinned La Indita, rather than the white Madonna of the Spaniards. (Indeed, the first Indians who venerated La Indita as the new mother still called her Tonantzin, the name of the Aztec mother goddess.)

Her hands are 'clasped' in a posture of prayer, and she is dressed in a long, rose-coloured robe with pale embroidery of gold, according to the royal Aztec custom. Her outer mantle is blue, patterned in stars, and she stands on a crescent moon of the first quarter, borne up by a winged angel. Around the whole image is a pearly white cloud.

The bishop was eventually convinced, and the first church was built: a rather rudimentary rectangular house in the Indian style – adobe, unburnt sun-dried bricks and a wooden roof.

Over the centuries this was enlarged and rebuilt several times in a desperate bid to cater for the ever-increasing number of pilgrims. In 1895 an enormous, ornate church was built in the Spanish Colonial style, with a central dome of gold, four towers, and gigantic Corinthian pillars supporting the roof. It was sumptuously decorated, using 60 tons of pure silver for the altar furnishings and other embellishments. There was also a vast golden reliquary, set high on an altar of bronze and marble, which held the original cloak imprinted with the image of La Indita. On her feast days a jewel-studded crown was placed on her head.

Guadalupe today

In 1976 a striking modern building, designed by Pedro Ramirez Vázquez, Mexico's celebrated architect, was built to accommodate the vast numbers of pilgrims.

There is no doubt at all about the importance of La Señora de Guadalupe to Mexico: she gave her Indians a sense of self-worth and national pride, and her pictures and statues are on display almost everywhere: in shop windows, on stamps, in cars, in every church and in most public buildings. She has even been declared by Pope Pius X (1903–14) to be the 'Empress of the Americas'.

Guadalupe is worthy of a pilgrimage for a wide variety of reasons other than the religious and devotional. There are all the attractions of Mexico: the weather, the people, the food, the dramatic landscapes, the remains of an ancient civilisation; and there is the Basilica of La Señora itself. Her old church has been turned into a better-than-average museum. There is a small chapel near the holy well that bubbled up at the spot where she appeared, and steps lead up to another chapel on top of the hill, where her roses bloomed.

She is there all the time, with the devout on their knees before her, but the main pilgrimage is on 11 and 12 December, the Eve and Feast Day, when there are exotic and exuberant festivities for kilometres along the route of processions and marches, singing and dancing in the streets, bands, fireworks, Indian warriors decked out in their feathered magnificence, and all manner of other happy celebrations, long into the warm night and the next morning.

Below: commemorative gold medals, trophies for the pilgrims who have reached their goal

IMAGES
OF MARY

·

BELIEVERS IN ANY aspect of the divine will usually wish to see what they believe in. People have always made 'graven images' of their gods and goddesses and likenesses of things in Heaven above or Hell beneath.

Early humans moulded the Great Mother Goddess in clay, or carved her out in chalk. The Babylonians, the Assyrians and the Egyptians erected gigantic statues of their gods. The Greeks fashioned marble into the smooth flesh of Aphrodite, and the Romans made their gods of bronze. Even Buddhists, those most unworldly of people, have created serenely beautiful images of the 'Other Than' for their shrines and temples.

Since the god of the Christians, like so many other gods, was made flesh, and 'dwelt among us', it is completely natural that Christians have always tried to see him as he was. Their churches and homes are 'signed' with his life and works and wonders in visual forms: crucifixes, statues and paintings.

Because of the Mosaic commandment against graven images, Jews regarded themselves as prohibited from being artists, or even employing them, so it is extremely unlikely that any of the early portraits of Jesus can be from life.

The first of these images were painted on the walls of the Catacombs in Rome, and date from the 2nd and 3rd centuries at the earliest. They were probably produced from the verbal

An image of the Madonna carved in chalk at Krakow

descriptions passed on from those who had seen him – rather like an artist depicting Wellington or Napoleon without ever having seen their faces.

However, as the Church grew in size and influence and spread into the Gentile world, where there was a strong artistic tradition, a supply of 'authentic' portraits began to appear from the busy workshops of Constantinople (now Istanbul). These were usually claimed to be by St Luke.

Christians have been particularly keen in their desire to see a true likeness of the Virgin Mary, the embodiment of so much of the best and most gentle in us. There is slightly greater likelihood that some of her portraits may be genuine: after the death of Jesus, she lived on for between 12 and 20 years, so several people must have seen, known and remembered her as the mother of the man so many were beginning to accept as Saviour.

St Luke's portrait

The idea that St Luke was an artist surfaced in the 6th century; the claim that he had painted a likeness of Jesus surfaced in the 7th, and that of Mary consenting to sit for him took another century to emerge. From then on, the tradition developed that Luke had portrayed Mary and the divine child, and that this picture had pleased her so much that she had

RIGHT: *Our Lady of Pepetual Succour, an image venerated at Rome, in the Church of St Alfonso*

ABOVE & BELOW: *the Chiesa Della Salute in Venice*

ordained that her blessing should always accompany it, wherever it went.

After the Assumption of Mary into Heaven, and desiring to spread her influence further, St Luke is said to have sent the portrait to his friend, the 'most excellent Theophilus', for whom he had written his gospel and the Acts of the Apostles.

It later came into the possession of Eudocia, wife of the Byzantine Emperor, Theodosius II (408–50), who presented it to his sister, Pulcheria, who was later canonised. In the 450s, Pulcheria built three churches in

Constantinople to honour the Mother of God, and placed St Luke's painting in the central and largest of them. There it was held in great esteem, and for a thousand years was the object of devoted veneration, until, in 1453, the Turks captured the city and destroyed the sacred icon.

However, copies are still preserved, all more or less similar. The image at St Alfonso in Rome is known as *The Mother (or Our Lady) of Perpetual Succour* and dates from the 14th century. It is painted on wood, and is a perfect example of theology being explained by visual imagery rather than words.

Our Lord in his infancy has a vision of his passion and death: the divine child, who has been sleeping in his mother's arms, has woken suddenly, and sees the Archangel Michael holding the spear, and the sponge on a reed. He quickly looks the other way, and sees the Angel Gabriel holding the cross and the nails. Wherever he looks, his sorrow is always before him. In his childish fright he jerks, so that his sandal becomes loose and begins to slip off. At the same time he tightly clasps his mother's right hand, and she draws him close to her in comfort and protection.

As a series of symbols it has great power, and if the physical appearance of Mary is less than realistic, that is beside the point: every detail tells part of the theological message. Mary does not glance down to comfort her child, but stares at us in reproach for being

the cause of his coming crucifixion. Her large, open eyes and small mouth signify that she saw and pondered much, yet spoke little, though always wisely. Believers can see spiritual meanings for as long as they have the need or the ingenuity.

The Church, on the evidence of miracles wrought and graces received, has pronounced the icon *Valde Miraculosa* (the Very Miraculous Image): it is attributed with cures, conversions, blessings and comfort.

ABOVE LEFT: mosaic of Mary and Jesus at Aya Sofya, Istanbul BELOW: jewelled icon of the Virgin of Smolensk, Russia

THE BLACK MADONNAS

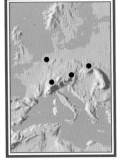

THERE ARE PROBABLY over 400 Black Madonnas in cathedrals and churches, isolated shrines, private collections and museums. As works of art they are not all of equal value: some are serene and beautiful, others badly painted or crudely restored – symbolic illustrations of doctrine, rather than representations of a real woman. Among the Black Madonnas enjoying particular esteem are those at Czestochowa in Poland, Einsiedeln in Switzerland and Mariazell in Austria.

In every case her face and hands are coloured black, or were once black. The Church attributes this to centuries of candle-smoke or chemical changes in the paint, and these parts have often been whitened in response to ecclesiastical demand. However, in most representations, the other colours have not darkened, and no single theory has ever been proved.

Poland

BELOW: Jasna Gora, in the Basilica of the Pauline Monastery

There is no doubting the fame and importance of the Black Madonna of Czestochowa, loved by Catholic Poles as the Queen of Poland. Her icon is venerated in the beautiful Marian Chapel of the Basilica of the Pauline Monastery as Jasna Gora (Bright Mountain), the national shrine and centre of Polish religious life. Over 300,000 pilgrims come to celebrate the Feast of Her Bodily Assumption into Heaven.

Nobody is quite sure where the icon comes from. As with so many relics, this was found by St Helena at Nazareth, taken to Constantinople, and eventually brought to what is now Poland, where the monks of St Paul of the Desert have kept it ever since. 'And all the victories and deliverances that have occurred since', writes Ean Begg in *The Cult of the Black Virgin*, 'are attributed by the Poles to the intercession of their patroness'. The list of perils, occupations and liberations is long: the Swedish, whose Lutheran troops slashed her face with sabres, Turks, Russians, Germans and Russians again after World War II.

Whatever the source of the original painting, the icon which exists today is an early 15th-century restoration by an unknown artist using the formal Byzantine style. Most of the surface is covered by an embossed sheet of jewelled silver-gilt, faintly tarnished, leaving only the faces and hands exposed. The sabre slashes can still be seen across her face. Many attempts have been made to repair these, but they have mysteriously reappeared. The faithful see this as a sign of Our Lady's sharing in the suffering of the world. Mary holds her baby in her left arm and gestures towards him with her right hand, while he blesses us with his right hand, and holds a small closed book in his left.

Switzerland

The National Shrine of Switzerland is in the abbey church of the Benedictines of Einsiedeln, Our Lady of the Hermits, where there is a famous statue of Mary as the Madonna of the Dark Wood, sacred to pilgrims since the 14th century. Just over a metre tall, she stands with the robed boy Jesus on her left arm; he holds a little bird in his left hand. Her dress is painted rich crimson and elaborately gilded, and over this she is usually clothed in the most gorgeous robes. The Swiss joke that she is the best-dressed Madonna in the whole world.

The name Einsiedeln means 'hermits', and the original hermit who lived on the site, situated in a high valley between Lake Zurich and Lake Lucerne, was a 9th-century monk called Meinrad who came to lead a solitary life of prayer in the mountain forests. He was eventually killed as a martyr in 861, and his miraculously preserved head is kept in a golden casket on which the Virgin stands in the black marble Chapel of Grace (Gnadenkapelle). Every year, on the day of his feast as a saint of the church, this relic is used to bless the people at Mass.

The abbey was established in the 10th century, but there have since been at least five terrible fires, and the present baroque building dates from the late 18th century. Pilgrims still come here from all over Switzerland, France, Germany, Italy and Spain.

There is a curious story about this particular Black Madonna. When the French

ABOVE: a copy of the Black Madonna of Czestochowa

invaded Switzerland and Italy in 1799 the soldiers were under orders from Napoleon to loot such relics and treasures, and thus, he hoped, weaken the power of the Roman Catholic Church. But the guardians at Einsiedeln substituted a replica, which was duly

WHEN unarmed workers shut and locked the gates of the Lenin shipyards in Gdansk, as part of the general strike which led to the collapse of the Soviet occupation, they hung a picture of the Black Madonna on the wire, as a sign of her protection.

FAR LEFT: the Black Virgin of Einsiedeln

sent back to Paris to be exposed as a fake. When, after the war, the genuine statue was returned by the monks who had looked after it in Austria, it had clearly been cleaned and repainted. So before being displayed again for the reverence of pilgrims, its traditional black hands and face had to be restored.

Austria

The most famous pilgrimage in Austria is to Mariazell, in the Styrian Alps, where there is an ancient limewood statue of a Black Madonna holding the boy Jesus on her left knee. According to the tradition this is the statue taken by a Benedictine monk called Magus when he left the abbey of St Lambrecht during the 12th century to join other hermits in the forests. The Virgin apparently helped him in a vision to find a suitable hermitage and he set the statue in a linden tree. A

small chapel was eventually built around this tree by shepherds and hunters. The chapel was later replaced by a larger one, and the shrine flourished over the years to become the religious focus of the old Austrian Empire.

Because of the many miracles and blessings believed to have been bestowed on her people, this Black Madonna is revered by pilgrims as 'the Great Mother of Austria' or 'the Lady of the Hungarians'.

Germany

An unusual Black Madonna is kept at Kevelaer, in Nordrhein-Westfalen, near the Dutch border: not a statue, but a copper-plate engraving which was printed at Antwerp during the 17th century. This is known to worshippers as 'Our Dear Lady, Consolation of Affliction', and a touching story is told about the beginnings of the shrine.

A peddlar called Hendrick Bussman was travelling along the road near Kevelaer when the Virgin spoke to him from Heaven giving him this request: 'Build a little chapel for me here.' She asked several more times during the next weeks, and he started to save enough money for materials. Then Bussman's wife had a vision of Mary with the boy Jesus as a picture which she could not afford to buy. Husband and wife saved even harder, and to their intense gratification soon found the engraving which matched the vision. They bought it and Bussman mounted it on a board and placed it in their new chapel. It is now the most important shrine in northwest Germany. Indeed, since a Papal Edict of 1949, this is, with Lourdes and Altotting, in Bavaria, one of the three European shrines dedicated to 'Our Lady, Queen of Peace'.

ROME

No matter what takes place there now, the intense reality of the past becomes an irresistible claim on submission and even affection.

(JOHN RUSKIN)

ABOVE: the wooden Throne of St Peter, in the apse of St Peter's Basilica in Rome

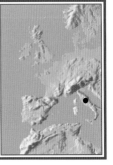

ALL ROADS LEAD to Rome, and when you arrive, it is overwhelming. There are so many names, dates, facts, sites and churches that a comprehensive pilgrim needs a degree in early Christian history, the latest edition of any standard guide and the 40 days of Lent, just to make a start. Careful selection is essential for a visit to be of any profit at all.

One church which would not necessarily be on a pilgrim's agenda, but which nevertheless reveals the soul of Rome in its name, is Santa Maria sopra Minerva. Known simply as the Minerva, it was built on the site of the temple dedicated to the Roman goddess of wisdom, a sign of the triumph of Christianity over paganism.

St Peter's

St Peter's is impressive even to those who are not Roman Catholic: all those creations of wood and stone, all that space and light and marble cladding, all those statues and inscriptions, the columns, the gilded plaster-work, shrines and altars. It is built, in fact, over a Roman necropolis – a 'city of the dead'

– with the authenticated bones of St Peter himself buried at the heart, under the papal altar and Michelangelo's towering dome. Peter is believed to have been crucified in AD 64 or 67 and to have been carried to this spot for burial by his followers.

In the apse, nearly insignificant within the most splendid reliquary ever devised, is the Throne of Peter, upheld by two Fathers of the Western Church, St Augustine and St Ambrose, and two of the Eastern, St Athanasius of the Creed and St John Chrysostom, surrounded by four gigantic serpentine pillars and topped by angels, clouds and rays from a golden halo and the dove of the Holy Spirit.

The throne is made of wood: pine, chestnut, oak and cypress. In 1968 carbon-dating showed the cypress to be the oldest (between the 4th and 6th centuries), and the others to date from the 10th and 12th centuries.

Simply to walk around St Peter's is to have the imagination stirred. Many pilgrims have seen eternity glimmering behind its ancient stained glass, or in the gesture of a worshipper making the sign of the cross as she kneels before Mary, or in the contrasts of the shadows of great columns and shafts of sunlight.

OPPOSITE (INSET AND MAIN PICTURE): Bernini's magnificent 17th-century baldacchino in St Peter's

THE FIRST KNOWN Church of St Peter, built in AD 326, was finally demolished in the early 16th century, having fallen gradually into a delapidated state. The new building – which was eventually to be the biggest church in the world – took well over 100 years to complete and involved the efforts of such masters as Bramante, Michelangelo and Bernini, and several changes of design along the way. St Peter's was consecrated in its new form on 18 November 1626.

THREE earlier churches stood on the site of San Giovanni in Laterano (see opposite) before being variously destroyed by Vandals, earthquake and fire. This was originally where the Pope resided; the Sancta Sanctorum (1278) is the only remaining part of the papal palace that was burned down in a fire of 1308.

RIGHT: San Giovanni in Laterano, the cathedral of the Bishop of Rome

Many are moved by the sight of the interior lit by hundreds of candles for Benediction of the Blessed Sacrament – though, these days, they are electric candles, and are all switched off at once, unlike the time when a long oak staff with a little brass cone on top was used to extinguish real candles one by one on the altar, the smoke pungent and lingering.

LEFT: Santa Maria Maggiore

San Giovanni in Laterano

San Giovanni in Laterano is the cathedral of the Pope in his position as Bishop of Rome. Inside, the Sancta Sanctorum, the Papal private chapel, used to bear the following inscription on the architrave of its altar: 'In the whole world no place is more sacred.' Its sanctity stemmed from the fact that it contained numerous relics, including the head of St Peter on the Gospel side, and the head of St Paul on the Epistle side (each in a reliquary of gold and precious stones), the Jewish Ark of the Covenant on a stand behind it, the holy Sprouting Almond Rod of Aaron, a golden urn full of manna collected from the wilderness, the tunic of Mary, part of the table of the Last Supper, a beam of the True Cross and a gold and jewelled crucifix filled with holy oil in which was said to be preserved the holy foreskin.

The Sancta Sanctorum remained open to pilgrims until the end of the 16th century, when it was looted by French soldiers, though the heads of St Peter and St Paul, without the valuable reliquaries, are still kept there behind a bronze lattice. Pilgrims are now permitted only to peer through a heavy iron grille into the dark.

They are, however, encouraged to ascend the 28 marble steps of the Scala Santa, the Holy Stairs, on their knees. These stairs, which lead from ground level to the closed chapel at the top, constitute the second largest Christian relic in the world, after the Holy House of Loreto. There are, of course, few things more poignant for the faithful than to climb the steps Jesus climbed to face Pilate. They were brought from Jerusalem by St Helena, first to Constantinople and later to Rome. They used to be outside, across the street. Pilgrims would climb them up to the door of a reception room at the top, where the Pope would bestow his blessing. They were moved to their present position late in the 16th century. Although the actual surface of the steps is protected from further wear by wooden boards, the pilgrims still continue to ascend, a prayer at a time.

Also preserved among the treasures of San Giovanni in Laterano is the slab of porphyry

LEFT: the Scala Santa (Holy Stairs) in San Giovanni in Laterano
ABOVE: pilgrims in the 1830s climbing the Holy Stairs on their knees

on which the Roman soldiers are said to have played dice for the seamless robe of Christ as he was hanging, naked, on the cross.

Santa Maria Maggiore

At the church of Santa Maria Maggiore lies buried the body of the 13th Apostle, Matthias who, after Christ's Ascension, was elected to replace Judas Iscariot. It also contains five pieces of wood from the manger in which the baby Jesus was laid: the Santa Culla, exposed for veneration at Christmas and the object of devotion of countless pilgrims. These are all that is left of a crib which had been kept intact from the 7th century until 1585, when Pope Sixtus V ordered its removal into the papal chapel. In the process the crib broke into pieces.

Santa Maria Maggiore is the biggest church dedicated to Mary in Rome and is a particularly impressive example of early Christian architecture – although several sections of it have been added and embellished in the centuries since its foundation.

THE STORY GOES that the church of Santa Maria Maggiore was built in AD 358 after Pope Liberius had a vision of Mary. She instructed him to build a church the following day wherever snow fell. This was in August – the height of summer – but it did snow, nevertheless, on the Esquiline Hill, and the church was duly built. Every year, on the anniversary of the vision (5 August), the Feast of Our Lady of the Snow is celebrated.

Santa Croce in Gerusalemme

The church of Santa Croce in Gerusalemme was first built in the 4th century, by order of the Emperor Constantine, to hold the relics brought back from the Holy Land by St Helena (see pages 38–9). Its treasures include a beam from the cross on which the Good Thief was crucified next to Jesus at Golgotha; three pieces of the True Cross; one holy nail; two holy thorns; stones retrieved from beneath the holy manger, and the index finger of Doubting Thomas, who thrust his hand into the wound in the side of the risen Christ.

There is also the *Titulus Crucis*, the inscription placed above Christ on the cross: 'Jesus of Nazareth, The King of the Jews', in Greek and Latin, painted on a wooden tablet, with the barest traces of Hebrew.

Santa Croce was rebuilt during the 18th century and again in the 1930s.

Santa Prassede

Near the altar in the church of Santa Prassede is a small pillar, often decorated with flowers. This is reputed to be the pillar of scourging to

ABOVE: Santa Croce

RIGHT: looking towards the altar of Santa Prassede

which Jesus was tied or chained, and was brought here from Jerusalem in the 13th century. The church is famous for its magnificent gilded Cappella di St Zeno, built by Pope Paschal for his mother.

San Lorenzo fuori le Mura

Surrounded by Rome's largest public cemetery, Campo Verano, San Lorenzo contains a chapel in which are imprinted two foot-marks made by Jesus, said to have been made when Peter was fleeing the persecution of Nero, and met Jesus on the road.

'*Quo vadis?*' he asked his master ('Where are you going?').

'To Rome', said Jesus, 'to be crucified again'. Peter was ashamed, and returned to his martyrdom. The foot-marks are imprinted in a basalt paving-stone from the Appian Way.

The church itself was built in AD 330 to commemorate another martyrdom: that of San Lorenzo, a deacon who was burned alive during the 3rd century. His crime was to present the ecclesiastical authorities with a crowd of poor people when asked to send the treasures of his church.

ABOVE: gilded decoration in the Cappella di St Zeno, Santa Prassede

San Paolo fuori le Mura

Built over the tomb of St Paul, this church contains his prison chains, which are displayed on his feast days. The present church dates from the 19th century; its predecessor burned down after workmen dropped hot coals and started a fire in 1823. It had survived since the 4th century, when it was built to accommodate growing crowds of pilgrims. The original church had been constructed on the orders of the Emperor Constantine.

Today's building was designed to reproduce the pre-1823 version, which was rich in decoration and mosaics. The fire was not the only catastrophe to hit San Paolo in its long history: it was also raided by Saracens in the mid-9th century and robbed of several tons of silver and gold treasures, as well as some, at least, of the contents of Paul's tomb itself.

BELOW: San Paolo fuori le Mura

ST PETER'S

THE BIGGEST CHURCH IN THE WORLD is the work of 10 architects and took 120 years to build, seeing out 20 popes. The original basilica of St Peter's, commissioned by Constantine (see pages 38–9), was the setting for imperial coronations and the target of barbarian raids: in 846 a Saracen attack led to the desecration of St Peter's tomb itself. Centuries of piecemeal restoration could not save the basilica from deterioration, and in 1503 Pope Julius II finally gave orders for a new church to take its place.

BRAMANTE AND GIULIANO DA SANGALLO were brought in to design a new St Peter's and in 1506 work started on Bramante's Greek cruciform plan, with a central dome and cupolas. By the time Bramante died in 1514 his ruthless demolition of the original basilica had earned him the nickname 'Destroyer', and the incomplete new building was the subject of fierce debate. For 30 years architects bickered, some favouring the addition of a twin-towered porch, others wanting to start all over again with a Latin cruciform design.

In 1547 Pope Paul III brought in Michelangelo, then in his 70s, who went back to Bramante's original plan but decided to make the dome much higher. For nearly two decades he worked on St Peter's for nothing, insisting on complete control of the project. When he died, in 1564, the transepts, the apse and the dome's drum and columns were finished. Giacomo della Porta completed the huge dome, raising it even higher than Michelangelo had planned.

Then, in 1606, everything changed yet again, when Pope Paul V decided he preferred the Latin cruciform design after all, and hired Carlo Maderno to carry out his wishes. The church was extended and its façade built before Maderno's death in 1629, and Bernini, his successor, set about tying up the threads of all the past designs. Under Bernini's direction St Peter's finally emerged as a baroque showpiece,

ABOVE: *the vast dome of St Peter's*

approached through a wide, colonnaded square (the Piazza San Pietro) and fronted by a long façade.

The interior

St Peter's is entered through a five-door portico, the central entrance having survived from the old basilica. Inside, the church houses 50 altars and 450 statues; its vast size is brought home by marks in the nave floor showing the extent of several other celebrated churches. In the first chapel along the right-hand aisle, Michelangelo's beautiful Pietà is displayed behind a screen (it was damaged by a vandal in the 1970s). The sculpture of Christ draped across Mary's lap was signed by Michelangelo (on Mary's gown) when rumours circulated that it was someone else's work. It is his only known signed piece.

Beyond the chapel are monuments to Queen Christina of Sweden, who abdicated in 1654 and converted to Catholicism, and to the Countess of Tuscany, the first woman buried in the church.

A 13th-century bronze statue of St Peter stands near the entrance to the crypt, its right foot worn down by the kisses of many thousands of pilgrims since 1857, when Pope Pius IX allowed 50 days of indulgence to Catholics showing their veneration in this way.

Bernini's bronze *baldacchino* (baldachin), or canopy, soars 29m above the high altar, crawling with bees, emblems of the arms of Urban VIII's family, the Barberini. Only the Pope can officiate at the altar, which is set above St Peter's tomb. The shrine itself was discovered in the second century; a headless skeleton was found there during excavations in the 1930s and '40s.

St Peter's Chair (Cathedra Petri), which dominates the apse, was made to hold the remnants of a throne apparently used by Peter and actually consisting of two seats in one: a 3rd- to 4th-century wooden chair within a 9th-century ivory coronation throne. Bernini's own sculpture is topped with cherubs and the dove of the Holy Spirit, extending its magnificent wings, nearly 2m across.

At the eastern end of the left-hand aisle is Alexander VII's melodramatic tomb, sculpted by Bernini in the 1670s and showing the Pope on his knees, summoned by the skeletal figure of Death, who beckons from behind swirling marble drapery.

Further west, the tomb of Innocent VIII is a rare survivor from the older church. Designed in the 15th century by Antonio del Pollaiuolo, it shows the Pope holding what some believe to be a fragment of the spear that pierced the side of Christ (see pages 36–7).

Just before the entrance of the church is a rather incongruous monument, dedicated to the last of the Stuarts of Scotland. Canova was commissioned by George III of Britain to produce this tribute to James, Charles and Henry Stuart – despite the fact that the Catholic Stuart dynasty, descendants of the deposed King James II, had claimed the right to occupy his throne.

LEFT: *a view of the cathedral's interior from the nave*
BELOW: *the high altar, protected by Bernini's 29m* baldacchino, *its carved bees a tribute to Pope Urban VIII*

SANTIAGO DE COMPOSTELA

In the Middle Ages Santiago de Compostela was one of the three major pilgrimages, along with Jerusalem and Rome. Pilgrims came here, to a remote north-western corner of Spain, to venerate the body of St James the Great.

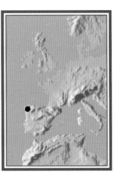

ST JAMES THE APOSTLE is remembered today as one of the brethren of Jesus, with family connections, and was a man of vital theological importance, as the leader of the First Synod of the Young Church in Jerusalem, in preference to St Peter and even St Paul. The settling of controverted doctrine, the hunting out of minor points of difference is no great inspiration to contemporary pilgrims, but to the medieval believers it was meat and drink, blood and fire, judgement and damnation. The site where St James' body was laid to rest had to be a place of power: this saint was not only brother to the Lord, but was also a Father of the Church, definer and teacher of the truth by which we are saved.

The history

According to believers, James' body is supposed to have been carried by angels from Jerusalem, where he had been beheaded, to this all but inaccessible spot, where it was found by a hermit who was led to the spot by a star. There was a modest stone tomb here, probably Roman (the name Compostela may derive from *compostum*, or burial place), and by the 8th century the then little town of Santiago de Compostela was already boasting that it contained the saint's remains.

Then a local bishop organised the building of a splendid cathedral to transform the tomb into a major shrine. His efforts bore fruit, and in 1478 Pope Sixtus IV put a pilgrimage to Santiago on the same spiritual footing as one to Jerusalem. This was probably for pragmatic reasons: due to various wars and invasions, Jerusalem was becoming more difficult for pilgrimages, but the Church did not want to lose the devotion of the faithful (not to speak of the revenue they provided for the custodians of relics and shrines).

'WHEN YOU be moved for to go your pilgrimage, and you know not the way, so ask it thus: "Good people, I go to St James at Compostela. At which gate of this city shall I go out? At which turn shall I take my way?"
And they shall tell: "On the right hand, when you come to a bridge, so go there over, and you shall then go a little way on the left hand, which shall bring you in a country where shall you see upon a church two high steeples. May God will you shall have a good journey." And so through that gate shall you go …'

A Phrase Book in French and English,
TRANSLATED BY CAXTON (1483)

ABOVE: the scallop shell signifies a successful journey to Santiago de Compostela
OPPOSITE PAGE: the magnificent main altar of the cathedral

ABOVE: *inside León Cathedral, on the pilgrimage route*

ABOVE: *Burgos Cathedral, south-east of León*

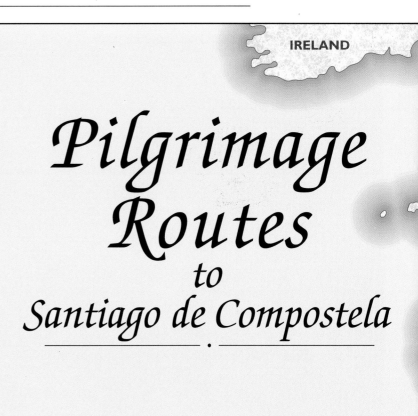

Pilgrimage
Routes
to
Santiago de Compostela

IRELAND

| 0 | 50 | 100 | 150 | 200 | 250 km |

La Coruña/
A Coruña

Cabo
Fisterra

**Santiago de
Compostela**

Gijón

Oviedo

Santander

Cordillera Cantábrica

GALICIA

Pontevedra

Vigo

Orense/
Ourense

León

Astorga

PORTO

Douro

CASTILLA

Burgos

Valladolid

Salamanca

Coimbra

PORTUGAL

S P A I

MADRID

Tejo

LISBOA

Badajoz

B a

B i

ST JAMES OF COMPOSTELA

ST JAMES, THE FISHERMAN and brother of John, became the first of Christ's Apostles to be martyred when King Herod Agrippa I ordered his execution in Jerusalem in AD 44. His connection with Spain dates from the 7th century, when stories began to circulate that he had visited the country to spread the gospel. Legend has it that his remains were brought back there and buried near Compostela, where they were discovered in AD 813.

ALTHOUGH NO EVIDENCE has ever been produced to back the claim that the bones, discovered in a stone coffin by a Galician peasant, are those of the saint, they were immediately proclaimed to be holy relics and enshrined. King Alfonso III had a church built over the spot in the early-10th century and Santiago soon became an immensely popular place of pilgrimage, drawing thousands of people from all over Europe. In 997 Al Mansur and his Muslim army ransacked the town and destroyed the basilica, but the faithful continued to make their way to the holy burial place.

By the 11th century Compostela was rated as highly by pilgrims as Rome and Jerusalem, and those who had made the arduous journey there wore their badge of achievement – the scallop shell – proudly on the brims of their hats.

In 1077 it was decided that a new and bigger cathedral was needed, and work started in July of the following year. Santiago was by far the most ambitious of the many churches built in Spain in the 11th and 12th centuries, and new working methods were introduced to tackle the project. The Master Builder, Bernard the Elder, is something of an enigma, but he is believed to have been a bridge builder who came from France, bringing with him a team of 50 stone-cutters. These masons were craftsmen, rather than quarrymen, who could fashion the stone to precise

ABOVE: *St James the Apostle*

instructions. The site architect, known to us only as Robert, assisted Bernard in his work, and the whole scheme was organised by the Master of the Chapter of Segeredo, Don Wicart, and the Abbot, Don Gundesindo. We know this much only because of the passing references made in Aimeric Picaud's guide book for pilgrims to Compostela, *Liber Sancti Jacobi*, written between 1139 and 1173.

A century after Bernard the Elder started work, the cathedral needed yet more rebuilding, and the task was undertaken by a Spanish architect, Master Mateo, between 1168 and 1188. Over the centuries, as more and more pilgrims followed the long and hazardous route to the shrine, new additions were made to the building to reflect its exalted status. During the 17th and 18th centuries it was covered in ornate baroque decoration, though the earlier interior was left alone.

The cathedral today

Of Santiago's three façades, looking out on to three plazas, the most notable is the sweeping baroque Obradoiro, designed by Fernando Casas y Novoa and flanked by slim towers. Behind it is Mateo's 12th-century Portica de la Gloria, a magnificent Romanesque creation covered with intricate carvings. Pilgrims mark their journey's end by touching the stone of the central pillar; innumerable fingers have worn a shallow groove into the column. The south transept entrance, the double-arched Puerta de las Paterías (Goldsmiths' Door), has fine carvings and statuary retrieved from the interior after a fire started by the townspeople in 1117.

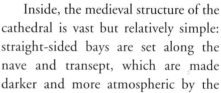

Inside, the medieval structure of the cathedral is vast but relatively simple: straight-sided bays are set along the nave and transept, which are made darker and more atmospheric by the lack of a clerestory (upper row of windows above the aisle roofs). Pilgrims process to the high altar, where stairs lead to a 13th-century statue of St James, whose cloak they kiss. The supposed relics of the saint and his followers, St Theodore and St Athonasius, are kept in the crypt below. Among the other church treasures are Antonio de Arfe's 16th-century gold treasure-pieces in the Reliquary Chapel and the wrought ironwork of the Mondragón Chapel.

On special occasions the large silver *botafumeiro*, or 'smoking tub', is suspended by a rope from the transept's central dome and swung by a team of eight men, trailing incense along the nave. The story goes that in 1588, during a ceremony to bless Philip II's Armada before its bid to invade Britain, the rope snapped and sent the incensory flying into the congregation – a fitting omen for the fleet, which was destroyed by the combined effects of English ships and a storm off the Hebrides.

LEFT: *a general view of Santiago de Compostela*
ABOVE RIGHT: *cathedral detail*
FAR LEFT: *16th-century pilgrims*

ABOVE: penitents with covered faces carry the cross

RIGHT: a statuette of the Virgin Mary, surrounded with flowers and candles, is carried by penitents into the church of Santiago

Nevertheless, the various routes to Compostela were hard going, the distances awe-inspiring on foot, the roads more often tracks. Robbers waited in the forests and mountain passes, cut-purses in the villages and towns; innkeepers were rapacious and nearly everybody was on the make: market traders, boatmen, toll-keepers charging extortionate fees to cross bridges; and then, when the pilgrim had finally arrived, there were the guides and fees and offerings. It took commitment and determination to make the journey at all, and in time the phrase 'the only true pilgrim', in the sense used by Dante to describe the 'journey through the days of this life', became reserved for one who had made the great pilgrimage to Santiago de Compostela.

The pilgrimage was big business, and surprisingly well organised, with inns and hostels along the way, 'official' leaders, priests, maps for sale, a guide published by the monks of Cluny for the use of pilgrims (warning of the dangers from thieves and overcharging) and even a phrase book in French and English, translated and printed by Caxton in 1483.

Slowly, over the years, four main pilgrim routes became established through France to Roncevaux in the High Pyrenees, some taking roundabout courses to pick up new travellers and avoid the more perilous country.

Pilgrims from England sailed out of the small ports along the east and south coasts, and made for the Valley of the Somme down to Amiens, and on to Paris, or for Le Havre and Rouen *en route* to Paris, where they would converge with those from Rheims who had come across from Germany.

From Paris they would troop south to Orléans and Tours, where others would join them from north-western France.

From Tours they would walk on, south to Poitiers and Limoges, with yet more travellers joining them from Bourges. The journey then continued to Conques, and on further to Rocamadour and Cahors.

The most southerly of the pilgrimage routes started at Lyon, came down the valley to Avignon and Arles and across to Toulouse – the Gateway to the Pyrenees – joining others at the famous Puente la Reine, the humpbacked bridge in Navarre.

Relics and preserved bodies and bones could be visited all along the way; almost every small town on the route had its own saint or miraculous statue – part of the head of John the Baptist, the body of St Mary Magdalene, and so on.

Finally, the pilgrims would make their way into Spain, walking westwards.

Other routes to Compostela led from northern Italy via Milan and Turin down to Avignon and Montpellier and Carcassonne. Through northern Spain they walked along the ridges of the Pyrenees to Pamplona, past the Sierra de la Demanda to Burgos, Astorgo. Others came up from Zaragoza, Madrid, Salamanca, Orense, Pontevedra – all walking on until they saw those distant towers.

ABOVE: pilgrims outside the cathedral in Santiago *BELOW LEFT: worshippers dressed in black arrive to celebrate Mass*

French monk Aimeric Picaud described the pilgrimage routes from France to Santiago de Compostela in the 12th century, in one of the world's first travel guides.

RIGHT: two contrasting representations of Mary and Jesus: a carved detail in the cathedral; and Christ being taken down from the cross

ABOVE: a notice in the cathdral gives times and details of the pilgrims' Mass

OPPOSITE PAGE: the cathedral's towering façade

These hundreds of thousands of pilgrims brought enormous prosperity to a region that had hitherto been desolate. Settlements that had once hardly existed as impoverished little towns soon had superb cathedrals and huge monasteries. The crowning glory was the Cathedral of Saint James in Santiago de Compostela, with its immense arched towers.

In the late-16th century it all changed. The war between England and Spain, the defeat of the Spanish Armada in 1588 and Francis Drake's attack on La Coruña, only a few kilometres away over the mountains, virtually closed down the shrine. The relics of St James were hidden to keep them out of the hands of the Protestant heretics, then lost. They were not found again until 300 years later. Eventually, with a little encouragement from the Church, the pilgrims started coming again, though in fewer numbers.

Compostela today

The end of World War II saw a renewal of this ancient pilgrimage, but with a difference: it is not to do with the veneration of dry bones but has everything to do with life. The point of the journey is not merely what the pilgrims find when they arrive, but also what they experi-

ence along the way: what they learn about themselves and the shared purpose of all the other pilgrims, communicating with strangers and becoming brothers and sisters.

Santiago is an archetypal pilgrimage, and to make it is to join all those others who have made it before. Medieval pilgrims brought back palms from Jerusalem to show that they had been there, and were called 'palmers'. From Santiago de Compostela they brought back a scallop shell. Nowadays pilgrims wear stickers to show who they are, where they come from, what they believe and where they have been.

The serious still start in Paris, or from one of the other traditional places in France, but they now set out equipped with walking boots, sticks and staves and detailed maps from the Spanish Tourist Board. They know exactly where to get their pilgrimage card stamped along the route to prove that they have actually walked and to qualify them for a certificate when they arrive.

In their own way and in their own time, for all manner of quite different reasons, these new pilgrims are on the road again, heading for another sort of Santiago de Compostela. Some see themselves as wandering scholars, with textbooks in their rucksacks; some as wandering minstrels, with stickered guitars.

They straggle along in a long line, as thunder rumbles in the distant mountains, between the gorse in full bloom, with the hawks hovering above and the road shimmering ahead. Sometimes they are overtaken by trucks with French, German or Italian television crews on board, carrying their cameras and microphones on long booms and preparing the latest documentary on pilgrims. The travellers walk on, past dry-stone walls, purple heather, wild flowers and bits of yellow plastic tied into the hedges at junctions to indicate the route. They stay in hostels along the way, served with local crab or prawns, steak and French fries, soup, bread and wine.

Eventually the towers of Santiago de Compostela appear, reached across a busy motorway. Medieval pilgrims would have approached the cathedral through the Porto do Camiño and down Calle Azbachería; now the route follows Rúa Nueva and the main street, Rúa del Villar, packed with shops and arcades; or Calle del Franco, leading past restaurants to the Renaissance Palacio de Fonseca, a university lecture hall.

The cathedral itself stands on the Plaza del Obradoiro, its impressive baroque façade topped by two towers. A good deal of the original 12th-century cathedral has been

preserved behind this elaborate façade, and a museum attached to the cathedral includes a fine exhibition of tapestries.

The Portico de la Gloria, dating from 1168, shows Christ and St James and hundreds of other figures, including those suffering in Hell. Pilgrims rest their hands on the central column while they rub their heads against that of the carver, Mast Mateo, himself portrayed in stone; the column bears witness to their homage, worn down with the impressions of their fingers.

The most important liturgical day is 24 July, the Feast of St James. The best time to arrive is on the evening before the feast day, when Mass is celebrated at the high altar in the cathedral. Some pilgrims pay their respects to St James on arrival by making straight for the high altar of alabaster, jasper and silver, which encloses his magnificent statue, regally seated and caped in yet more silver, encrusted with diamonds. The weary travellers climb the flight of stairs behind him on their knees and do their best to embrace him. After Mass they usually set out to get a meal somewhere, and at about 11.30pm there is a magnificent display of fireworks in the Plaza del Obradoiro, which is packed with a happy, cheering crowd.

The next morning, to crown the whole experience of the pilgrimage, many travellers catch a bus to travel the few kilometres to Cape Finisterre and further westwards to the place which was called *Finis Terrae* by the Romans – the End of the Earth. There, they walk up the hill from the village to the Atlantic Ocean, with nothing before them except salt water and America.

NAPLES

The liquefaction of St Januarius' blood was described by St Aloysius in the 16th century: 'The previously solid, dark brown mass, during an interval of not more than 25 minutes, became perfectly liquid and at the same time ruby red in colour, like freshly shed blood.'

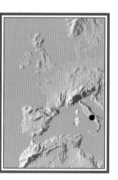

*T*HE STORY of St Januarius, patron saint and protector of Naples (Napoli), dates back to the early years of the 4th century and was first reported in the middle of the 6th century. As a young man Januarius was converted to Christianity, and eventually became a bishop. The story goes that he fell foul of the local Governor of Campania, and was sent to the arena of Pozzuoli to be savaged by wild beasts. However, none of these beasts would lay a claw on him, so he was beheaded.

A century later Januarius' body was exhumed by Christians, and they were astonished to discover that it had not corrupted, and that his congealed blood began to flow (though this phenomenon was not reported until nearly a thousand years later). Prudently, they collected as much as they could of the blood in glass bottles, and preserved them and the body in a small church.

Everything was removed from the church for safe-keeping during the wars with the French, but in 1294 the Neapolitan church authorities ordered the building of a great cathedral dedicated to this martyr and saint, long regarded as the protector of the city.

Two centuries later, the body of Januarius and the bottles of his blood were carried in triumph to a shrine in the cathedral, where they are venerated to this day.

The shrine today

The saint's body now rests in the crypt, but his head, which had been hacked off at the neck, is kept in a bust of silver gilt, in a tabernacle behind the main altar of a magnificent chapel. His blood is in two crystal phials on either side, one larger and almost full, the other almost empty.

There is a huge grille of gilded bronze in front of the chapel, and a balustrade designed to protect the altar of the blood inside.

Several times a year, as a sign that he is still bestowing his favours on the city, the saint's congealed blood liquefies.

Some believers are persuaded that the speed with which the blood liquefies indicates how much prosperity St Januarius will bestow on Naples. Every so often, especially on various anniversaries in May, September and November, vast crowds gather in and around the cathedral, the head is exposed for veneration on the altar, the people pray and the archbishop shakes the larger of the two phials, and brings it closer to the head. If all goes well, the black liquid turns red, and sometimes froths. The archbishop then turns towards the congregation and announces: 'The miracle has occurred!' At this the people sing and wave thousands of fluttering handkerchiefs in the air.

RIGHT: the Piazza del Plebiscito

Father Herbert Thurston of the Society of Jesus, a scholar who also had grave doubts about the Shroud of Turin (see pages 40–1), made a 'thorough investigation' of all the available evidence, and refused to believe that this was the actual blood of the saint. He had to admit one disturbing fact, however: 'Few, if any, alleged miracles have been examined more carefully, more often, or by people of more divergent views … and it may be safely affirmed that no expert inquirer, however rationalist in temper he may be, now denies that what is said to take place does take place' (*The Catholic Encyclopaedia*, 1909).

The blood of St Januarius has never, in fact, been properly tested. In 1972, under public pressure, the then archbishop gave his consent to a 'scientific examination'. A lecturer in anatomy, who had published several treatises in defence of the miracle, was to direct the work of a hæmatologist, a psychologist and a parapsychologist. But the phials were not to be opened. In effect, all they could do was to view the substance through inch-thick antique crystal. Lack of scientific proof of the blood's authenticity does not worry the Neapolitans. This is not about science but about faith, and all the various pilgrimages to witness the liquefaction are exuberant occasions, to be enjoyed for all manner of reasons.

The cathedral, in the centre of the Old Town, is undoubtedly a master work in the French Gothic style, and the sumptuous crypt is typical of the Italian Renaissance, with its ornate bronze doors, florid marble, gold and silver embellishments and altar furnishings.

Modern Naples

Naples itself, glutted with palaces and churches, has a flamboyant beauty and a lifestyle in which religion is ever-present. A walk through the streets reveals glass-fronted, candle-lit shrines at nearly every corner; even the prostitute makes a quick sign of the cross in gratitude as she gets into the car of the man who has picked her up. Their religion', according to one Neapolitan Franciscan, 'is their life – not something they save for Sundays'.

BELOW: the Chapel of San Gennaro by Gigante Giacinto (1806–76)

ASSISI

Now one of the most popular and best-loved saints, Francis of Assisi attracted a wide public following and the blessing of the Pope in his mission to bring simplicity and humility back to Christian life.

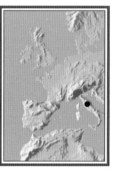

SINCE 1860, when knowledge of St Francis was more widely disseminated, the birthplace of the ascetic 'Little Brother' and the centre of his religious order has drawn countless Protestant and Catholic pilgrims.

The history

Francis was born Giovanni di Bernardone in 1181, the young son of a wealthy merchant draper. He was, to quote his own words, 'ignorant and unschooled', and spent most of his youth in the company of a crowd of frivolous pleasure-seekers, doing nothing in particular.

Early one February morning, at the beginning of the 13th century, Francis was attending Mass when the priest read the words of Jesus to the disciples: 'Go, preach, saying, the Kingdom of Heaven is at hand. Provide neither gold, nor silver, nor coins in your purse, nor pack for your journey, neither two coats, neither shoes, nor yet staves ...'

Francis took these words of Jesus to heart. He stripped off his clothes and stood naked before his God. He subsequently started his Order of Barefoot Brothers, who would go forth similarly stripped of all their worldly goods, on a mission to bring men and women to God and righteousness.

Even Roman Catholic apologists admit that the Church was corrupt, rich, rigid with dogma, embroidered with incomprehensible doctrines and a formidable political force, its hands bloody with the making and breaking of kings and emperors. With the ascendancy of Pope Innocent III (1198–1216), the temporal power of the Church was at its zenith. The Pope had fathered several illegitimate children, known as his 'nephews' and 'nieces', and exerted a good deal of his energy on the pursuit of gastronomic and artistic excellence, matched only by his zeal for collecting works of art.

Many of the faithful were disillusioned and ready to lend their support to any effective 'new broom' that came along – though Francis of Assisi was an unlikely figure-head for any zealous march against ecclesiastical authority. Indeed, he had no wish to oppose the Church, and insisted on obedience to the Papacy. This approach allowed the Pope to give his blessing to the Franciscan Order and to keep this potentially threatening alternative to established religion within the fold.

Francis was a small, dark-skinned man, with eyes like black olives, the stubble of a beard, dirty, unkempt and haggard (though hagiographies present him as the tenderest and sweetest of Christian saints, give him the affectionate nickname of 'Little Pauper', and claim that little flowers sprang up wherever he

ABOVE: St Francis shown preaching to birds in a 1920 stained-glass window in Selborne Church, Hampshire

ABOVE: the ostentatious Assisi church dedicated to St Francis, who preached simplicity and humility

walked). He was, nevertheless, a man of great personal charm and magnetism, who attracted affection and loyalty among his followers, the 'Little Brothers' and among the dwellers of towns and cities where he took his message, alternating his urban ministry with periods of meditation in his hermitages.

His strong personality has ensured that, even through the stained-glass biography written 'under obedience' by Brother Bonaventura 35 years after Francis' death, we can glimpse the man of all too human flesh and blood, struggling not only with the Church but with the demands of spiritual warfare against carnal sin.

Torn by the opposing desires of soul and body, Francis was driven to mortify the flesh: he ate 'but little food, and that of the meanest', even sprinkling it with ashes to destroy the taste; hardly ever drank, even when 'parched with burning thirst' (*The Little Flowers of St Francis*, Bonaventura).

Having cast aside all material goods, he continued his search for the means of more

ABOVE: the vaults of the Lower Church in the Basilica di San Francesco

follow this by flinging himself on to thorns for the sin of enjoying the lash.

Francis himself said that 'one who so much as spoke to a woman could as little avoid contamination therefrom as he could walk upon burning coals and his feet not be burned'. Yet his Order included a 'Little Sister', Lady Clare. It is said that as soon as she heard of him, she could not rest until she had come to him, and that to him she had opened her heart. Then after she had received from him many holy words, he exhorted her above all other things to flee the world, both with her heart and with her body. He enjoined her that on Palm Sunday she should turn her joy into weeping and afflictions, for by lamenting the Passion of Christ she would finally reach Heaven as a virgin.

So Lady Clare went to the Altar of the Blessed Virgin Mary, where her hair was cut off, and she was espoused the Bride of Jesus, and went to live with her companions in holy poverty, fed simply and clothed with only one poor coat, never without knotted horsehair next to her naked flesh. For a pillow she took a block or a great stone, and she lay on the bare ground, until eventually she died.

On Holy Cross Day, 14 September 1224, before dawn, Francis began to contemplate the Passion of Christ, and his fervour grew so strong that he became 'wholly transformed into Jesus through love and compassion'. Then, after a long period of secret conversation, an image of the Passion of Jesus Christ appeared on his body – the marks of the nails

BELOW: St Clare and her life pictured in the church which marks her burial place, Santa Chiara

rigorous abstinence: 'The bare ground for the most part served as a couch unto his wearied body, and he would often sleep sitting, or with a log or stone placed under his head.' In the winter, he would plunge into a ditch full of snow, 'that he might both utterly subdue the Foe within him, and might thus preserve his White Robe of Chastity from the Fire of Lust.'

Whenever he felt in danger of succumbing to temptation of the flesh, he would scourge himself with a knotted cord – only to

ABOVE: a view of the ancient town of Assisi

OPPOSITE PAGE: Francis' simple home, Porziuncola, now standing in the church of Santa Maria degli Angeli and covered in rich decoration

and the mark of the spear: the stigmata. They never left him, continuing to cause him suffering and pain.

In 1226, when he was sure that he was dying, Francis asked that he be laid naked on the earth, where he was left by his followers, very calm and quiet and staring up towards the sky. He died late on a Sunday, while a 'great multitude of meadow larks came on the roof of the hut where he lay, and, flying about, made a wheel around the Heavens, sweetly singing, praising the Lord'.

Assisi today

The landscape of Umbria is serene, and the little town of Assisi, nestling on the slopes of Mount Subiaso, seems like a large mural painting, doing its best to live up to its history as the background to the life of Francis. Since the saint was born here it has hardly changed, and its ancient character has helped to preserve his cult. Little, winding, stone-paved streets, lined with old houses, lead from the base of the town to its various monuments.

Guide books mention the Corinthian portico of the temple of Minerva as evidence of Assisi's existence in Roman times, and offer the cathedral and the great 14th-century fortress, built by Cardinal Albornoz above the ridge, as proof of its medieval importance. But apart from its association with Francis, Assisi is just a standard entry in the guide books, worth a visit along with

BELOW: Assisi's association with St Francis is in evidence all over the town

other places of interest on the tourist route. Francis himself has made this holy land – because, of all Christians whose lives are as well documented, he seems to be the one who lived closest to the ideals of his Master, albeit within the theological conventions of his own day.

Francis built, with his own hands, a small rock shelter, which he referred to as his Porziuncola, the 'Little Portion', in which to retreat from the world. Here he could be alone to pray, meditate and achieve contemplative union with God. Over this retreat, and over the place of his death, the Pope erected what various other critics have called the 'arrogant', the 'totally insensitive', the 'gross', the 'almost blasphemously over-bearing' church of Santa Maria degli Angeli, in an attempt to make holy what was already holier than anything the masons could possibly create with their hands.

There is no denying the beauty of the fresco paintings of Giotto. His lovely images, created towards the end of the 13th century, include a representation of the encounter between Francis and his followers and the powerful Pope Innocent III, and may be seen by many as wholly worthy tributes to Francis' life.

Yet merely to be at Assisi at all is to experience the presence of the Little Brother: this is where he lived and these are the places that he loved. Set in the cloister of the monastery built in his name is the Roseto, the rose garden in which he fought that useless fight against the flesh by tearing himself on their thorns. Here, it is said, the very roses shed their thorns in pity for him, and have to this day remained thornless.

Buried in the crypt of her church in Assisi, Santa Chiara, is the body of Francis' devoted follower, Lady Clare, incorruptible behind glass, with the flowers always fresh in her hands. Near by are her undergarments and some of the blonde curls cut off by Francis when he espoused her the 'Bride of Jesu'; next to them is the worn tunic of Francis himself.

Her sisters, the Poor Clares, sell simple prayer-cards, decorated with pressed wild flowers from the fields around Assisi.

COLOGNE

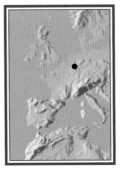

OPPOSITE PAGE: busts of the virgins displayed on elaborate shelves in the Church of St Ursula

COLOGNE (KÖLN), set on the Rhine, is a magnificently beautiful city, with a cathedral considered to be one of the most important Gothic churches in Europe. It took 600 years to build – from the 13th to the 19th centuries – following the preserved designs of its medieval architects. It boasts two impressive steeples, delicate stonework, a beautiful 15th-century altarpiece and the fine golden shrine of the Magi, the last resting place of the crowned corpses of the Three Kings, who brought their gifts of gold, frankincense and myrrh to the baby Jesus.

Cologne is still a city of churches, even after the devastation of its centre in World War II, including 12 exquisite Romanesque examples. Pilgrims come here principally to visit the Church of St Ursula, and to venerate her bones and those of her companions.

BELOW: an exterior view of the Church of St Ursula

The history

There are various versions of the story of Ursula, ranging from the middle of the 3rd century to the end of the 5th. She may have been the daughter of an early Cornish or British king; in some accounts she was a queen in her own right. With 11 companions she set sail to found a new colony in Brittany, but the ship was caught in a storm and wrecked on a strange shore, where the women were raped and butchered by barbarians. In other versions Ursula was promised in marriage to a ferocious tyrant, who threatened to lay waste her father's lands unless she consented, but she begged a delay of three years to sail the high seas with 11 virgins as companions, each with a thousand virgins in attendance, in 11 ships. A storm drove them into the mouth of the Rhine, from which point they made their way down the river to Cologne and Basle, disembarked and walked over the Alps on a pilgrimage to meet the Pope in Rome – only to be killed by the Huns on their way back.

The bodies of Ursula and her companions were somehow collected and taken to be buried in a Roman cemetery at Cologne. Their remains were exhumed during the 12th century and transferred to the exquisite church that had been built in order to house them.

The shrine

During the Middle Ages, at a time when consecrated celibacy was greatly respected, St Ursula was extremely popular, and a sought-after source of relics. (As late as the 16th

ABOVE: bones of the
virgins, carefully arranged
in intriguing patterns
ABOVE RIGHT: Ursula
with the ship that carried
her to martyrdom

RIGHT: St Ursula's skull,
kept safe in its ornate
reliquary

century, the Jesuits were smuggling various parts of her body to Lisbon.) But behind the high altar of the Church of St Ursula in Cologne, in a jewelled shrine, the rest of her remains are kept, and on either side of them are the busts of two of her virgin followers – each one hollow, so that you may view the bones that are lodged there in red velvet. More busts gaze down on visitors from their vantage points on high.

The Golden Chamber is a square chapel elaborately decorated with more busts, human bones and gold than are ever likely to have been gathered in one place before. There are several shelves of them: some busts are made with lids that can be opened to snatch a glimpse of the skulls kept inside; glass cupboards contain other skulls carefully arranged on embroidered red cloth, and thousands more bones are arranged high up on the walls above, in curiously inventive patterns.

Under the altar there are even more busts, and, behind it, kept in a glass reliquary, is the surprisingly small skull of St Ursula herself. It is here that the devout come to kneel in tribute to this martyr, cloaked in mystery.

IRISH SHRINES

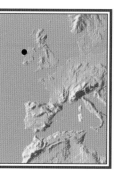

IRELAND IS A land of intense religious devotion, with a long history of sectarian conflict. It celebrates a bewildering number of saints; shrines and candles are a common sight on roadsides and in houses. Some of the Irish saints are well known far beyond their homeland. St Columba, born in Donegal in AD 521, left the country in 563 to spread the word of God from the Scottish islands (see pages 122–4); St Brendan the Navigator, who sailed the Atlantic Ocean in search of paradise during the 6th century, took the Christian message to western Ireland and founded a monastery in Clonfert, County Galway. But the most famous saint of all must surely be St Patrick, Ireland's patron saint.

St Patrick

Born in about AD 385, Patrick was the son of a Roman official posted to Britain and living near the Severn estuary. At 15 or 16 he was seized by Irish raiders and held captive in Ireland, where he made friends with the local children and learned to speak Gaelic. He was then sold as a slave to an Irish chieftain and worked for six or seven years as a shepherd on Slemish Mountain in County Antrim.

During his captivity Patrick began to take an interest in religion and to pray regularly. He finally managed to escape to the coast and obtain passage on a ship to France, where he studied for the priesthood for another six or seven years. After this he had a dream in which he was summoned back to Ireland to bring the natives to Christ, and he duly returned in about 432.

Although Christianity already had some followers in Ireland, it was Patrick who did most to spread the gospel – working mainly in Ulster, Leinster and Connacht. He confronted the High King of Tara, Laoghaire, in 433 by disobeying his command and lighting the paschal, or Easter, fires on the Hill of Slane – thus establishing a formidable reputation among the high and mighty of the land.

In his last days, it is said, Patrick retreated to the Mountain of Croagh, carrying a great bell in his hand, and prayed on the highest reach there for 40 days and 40 nights, with no food or drink. Then he wrested a promise from the angels that Ireland would keep the holy faith until the second coming of Christ.

Patrick then hurled his great bell down the chasm on the side of the mountain, and the angels tossed it back for him to hurl it down again, driving the serpents and demons away with the fearful disturbance.

Croagh Patrick today

The climbing of that Holy Mountain in late July is the greatest pilgrimage of all Ireland, with as many as 50,000 people taking part.

The mountain is a cone of quartz and shale, rising on the southern side of Clew Bay on the Atlantic coast of County Mayo.

ABOVE: St Brendan the Navigator, a 6th-century sailor in search of paradise

Pilgrims make the gentle approach to Croagh Patrick over flat fields, some barefoot, most wearing stout shoes, following the track up through the heather of the first slopes, on uneven and soggy ground, before tackling the winding, steep ascent, with its sharp stones and heaving boulders, and the narrow ridge with a grand view of purple mountains across the southern valleys. Finally they complete the breathless climb of the cone itself.

The bare and bruised feet of a Croagh Patrick pilgrim

ABOVE: kneeling at the altar in Knock
RIGHT: St Patrick's statue at Croagh

Knock

This village on a gentle rise of pasture in County Mayo, about 30km east of Croagh Patrick, was the scene of a famous vision in the late 19th century. On a wet Thursday night in August, 15 witnesses claimed to have seen the Virgin Mary, motionless, raised slightly above ground level, with her back to the southern wall of the parish church. With her, on either side, were St Joseph and St John the Evangelist, and near them was an altar, on which were a lamb and a cross. They hovered there in silence for two or three hours.

Stories circulated that it was all done with a magic lantern, and the young assistant priest was caught trying to duplicate the vision on the end wall of his next church a few years later. A nun who was at first convinced, and founded a convent on the site, later dismissed it all as a fictitious miracle. But the first cure was reported 10 days after the vision, and there were 100 more by the spring of the following year. The pilgrims began to hack bits of cement off the gable wall, dissolving them in holy water and drinking the concoction to ward off disease and affliction. When the cement had all been shared out, they took the mortar, leaving the stones to collapse – so the wall had to be repaired and shored up, to prevent the whole church from falling down.

The grand concrete Basilica of Our Lady Queen of Ireland now stands at the site, attracting half-a-million pilgrims a year. Inside, the 32 pillars in the ambulatory were contributed by all the counties in the country and the four windows in medieval style represent the four provinces of Ireland. At the end of the gable, a glass box contains the three statues of the vision, made of Carrara marble imported from Italy.

Knock's finest hour came in 1979 when Pope John Paul II visited in its centenary year.

Thousands of pilgrims of all ages, shapes and sizes struggle up the mountain, slipping, clambering on their hands and knees, passing others who are coming down and who assure them that it is not far to the top, until there, finally, is the Atlantic Ocean, shimmering like a shield of hammered bronze, and the final summit, where Mass is being said.

Here, with the mountains to the south, the broad lands to the east, the scattered islands of Clew Bay below and the great dreaming island of Clare out to the west in the waves of the Atlantic, pilgrims come for a glimpse into another world.

RIGHT: the Basilica of Our Lady Queen of Ireland at Knock, County Mayo

Saint Patrick's Purgatory

The most intense pilgrimage in all Ireland, possibly in the whole of Christendom, is one of repentance and self-inflicted pain, set among magnificent scenery. The mountains of Galway and County Clare lie over to the west, and the island that attracts such devotion – Station Island, east of Donegal – rises from the grey-green waters of Lough Derg, the largest of the lakes along the River Shannon. A few buildings have been built on it, and a pier has been constructed for landing.

Legend has it that pilgrims have been coming from all over Europe since the 12th century at the earliest, certainly from the early 17th. Thousands still come every season from the beginning of June to the middle of August, hundreds at a time taking the short boat trip out to the island for a stay of three days, which requires booking and paying a small charge for lodgings.

Purgatory is the place and state in which souls not ready for Heaven at death suffer a purging process of purification before entering into the joy of their redemption. Many of Ireland's faithful hold that this pilgrimage offers the only genuine opportunity of reducing the time spent in Purgatory by doing serious penance on earth – penance being an action performed by a believer to show repentance and reparation for sin. Specific conditions are required on the part of the penitent: sorrow for one's sins; a firm purpose of amendment or resolution to avoid all sin or the likely occasions of sin; the confession of sins to a priest; his granting of absolution or the spiritual washing clean by forgiveness; and the performance of the penance the priest imposes – usually saying certain prayers.

Pilgrims come here in commemoration of Patrick's 40 days of prayer and fasting, and suffer their own privations. The rules are simple: bare feet, one meal a day, no smoking, no alcohol, Mass every morning at dawn,

the rosary at regular intervals, a night spent in sleepless vigil, personal devotions, examination of conscience, confession and holy communion.

ABOVE: pilgrims gather at the Ballinspittle grotto to see the moving statue

The Dancing Virgin of Ballinspittle

Ballinspittle, whose name is Gaelic for 'the mouth of the ford for the hospital', is a small village south-west of Cork. It has been a shrine of pilgrimage since two women took a walk up the lane to the grotto, shortly before the Feast of the Assumption not long ago. There are many such grottoes all over Ireland, usually based on the grotto at Lourdes. In the Ballinspittle grotto there is a painted statue of Mary, with a halo of 12 electric light bulbs as the stars of her crown.

As the two women stood praying in the twilight, the statue moved, swaying back and forth. The harder they looked, the more obvious was the movement. The following night there were 40 pilgrims at the grotto, and most agreed that the statue was moving. By the end of the week a thousand people a night were in procession up that lane, a field was converted into a car park, and there was a steady trade in hot-dogs and fish and chips from enterprising vans.

On the Feast of the Assumption, 15 August, 20,000 people assembled from all over Ireland, many with cameras to record the miracle, and the statue was seen to sway to and fro, and from side to side, with hands parting and head rocking.

The church is preaching prudence and caution, and maintaining that all natural explanations will have to be examined before a conclusion can be reached. Meanwhile, the shops and pubs of Ballinspittle are doing a great trade, and pilgrims are flocking there to satisfy their hunger for mystery and miracles.

LEFT: prayers are offered to the Dancing Virgin of Ballinspittle, near Cork

CANTERBURY

Famed for the unique and vivid characters portrayed in Geoffrey Chaucer's fictional pilgrimage in the 14th century, Canterbury has seen countless thousands of men and women make the annual journey to the shrine of St Thomas à Becket.

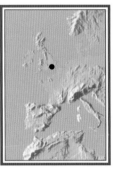

ONE OF the most famous pilgrimages of them all no longer takes place. Its most celebrated description was made by Geoffrey Chaucer in his satirical poem, *The Canterbury Tales* during the 14th century, when it was, along with the shrine at Walsingham (see pages 115–17), the most popular pilgrimage in Britain – and possibly in the whole of medieval Europe.

The journey from London to visit the shrine of the 'holy blissful martyr', St Thomas à Becket, at Canterbury Cathedral, continued to attract huge crowds of travellers from all walks of life for the following two centuries.

In the spring, groups of people from all over the country would arrive, as did Chaucer's pilgrims, at a well-known hostel in south London: the Tabard at Southwark. In the *Tales*, they arrange to travel on together, 'some nine and twenty in a company', and, 'early next morning at the spring of day', they set out along the Old Kent Road. The pilgrims put up at a different inn every night and ride the 70 or so miles to Canterbury in four-and-a-half days.

Chaucer's main concern was not the spiritual side of the pilgrimage itself, nor with the

Pilgrims in the 13th century, shown in a stained-glass window in Canterbury Cathedral's Trinity Chapel

religious activities at the famous shrine, but rather with the pilgrims as characters and the tales they tell to entertain the company on their journey: tales of high romance between noble lords and fair ladies, of sexual farce and unscrupulous seduction, of greed, gluttony, corruption, religious and commercial fraud, and so on.

Among the rather mixed company of pilgrims are a villainous mercenary soldier, who has taken part in some of the most pitiless slaughters of recent wars, yet who 'loves chivalry' and 'courtesy'; a mincing prioress, who cares more for her table manners and for 'speaking daintily in French' than for anything else; a fat monk who dines on roast swan and 'loves the hunting of the hare'; a wanton friar who sells 'forgiveness for good money' and 'spurns the poverty-stricken poor'; a rapacious lawyer who 'exacts large fees'; a doctor who 'counts the gold he gains from pestilence'; a poor country priest; a ploughman; a miller; another nun; and a widow who has had 'five churched husbands' in all and 'several men of her youth', and who has already been on seven previous pilgrimages, including no fewer than three to Jerusalem.

Chaucer is thus describing not only the

THE BODY of Thomas à Becket was not the only attraction at Canterbury Cathedral: the cathedral also possessed the complete bodies of St Alphege, St Anselm and St Dunstan, with the heads of three other saints and the arms of 11 more, a large piece of the True Cross, a thorn from the holy crown, wool woven by Mary, a leg from the cradle of the baby Jesus, Aaron's rod and some of the clay from which God made Adam.

OPPOSITE PAGE: the altar, Canterbury Cathedral

CHAUCER
AND THE
CANTERBURY TALES

WHEN GEOFFREY CHAUCER BEGAN WORK on the *Canterbury Tales* in 1387 he was a well-travelled man who had seen much of medieval society, high and low. The son of a wine merchant, he had served as a soldier, diplomat and courtier, as well as earning international fame as a prolific writer and translator. He began this final work as a widower in his middle age, looking back over his own full career and casting an eye on the world around him. Hypocrisy, lechery, corruption and greed were all captured in his vivid portraits – as were compassion, loyalty and, above everything, a joyous love of human life, warts and all.

BORN BETWEEN 1339 and 1346, Chaucer went to live with a noble family and was sent as a soldier to France, where he was taken prisoner and ransomed. Having entered the king's court he met his future wife, Philippa de Roet, a lady-in-waiting related to John of Gaunt, who became Chaucer's life-long patron. Chaucer rapidly climbed the career ladder, serving as a royal diplomat in France, Genoa, Lombardy and Florence, before being appointed the controller of customs in the port of London.

The pilgrims and their tales

Chaucer had probably seen pilgrims on their way to Canterbury – the package-holidaymakers of their day – and may have joined them after his wife's death in 1387.

ABOVE: the Nun's Priest

This was the year in which he wrote the General Prologue of the *Canterbury Tales*, introducing the 'nyne and twenty … sondry folk' who gather at the Tabard Inn in Southwark and agree to travel together. Harry Bailly, the host of the Tabard, suggests a story-telling competition. Each pilgrim must tell four stories – two on the way there, two on the way back; the best tale-teller wins a free dinner at the inn.

Chaucer's work was unfinished when he died in 1400, and only 24 stories are told (Chaucer himself tells two). Linked with snatches of dialogue, they combine with the lively individual portraits presented in the Prologue, to offer a fascinating glimpse of 14th-century life.

The **Knight**, who travels with his young son, the Squire, is a war-weary soldier who has seen action in Prussia, Alexandria, Granada and

North Africa, and who comes fresh from an expedition, his tunic spattered with chain-mail rust. This 'verray parfit, gentil knight' has generally been taken at face value, as noble and courageous – but recent interpreters suggest that Chaucer's sense of irony has been passing us by.

The drunken **Miller**, a stout bagpipe-player with a wart on his nose, offends the **Reeve** (who practises carpentry) with his story of a cuckolded carpenter. In return the Reeve, 'a sclendre, colerik man', entertains the company with a tale of an unscrupulous miller who robs two clerks of their flour: his victims take their revenge by sleeping with the miller's wife and daughter.

Further hostilities are played out in the **Friar**'s account of a summoner who deals with the devil and is carried off to hell; and in the **Summoner**'s own story of a greedy friar who earns a legacy to his community of 'a fart'. These two unsavoury characters are well matched: Hubert, the grasping, lisping Friar who can persuade even the poorest widow to part with her money; and the lecherous, scabby Summoner, who loves strong wine, onions and leeks, and speaks only Latin when he is drunk.

The **Cook**, who has come along 'To boille the chiknes with the marybones', has his own tale of an apprentice and a prostitute cut short – perhaps because it follows two other earthy stories and even Chaucer decides to draw the line. The gap-toothed, partly deaf **Wife of Bath**, who has seen off five husbands and is on the lookout for a sixth, is an

ABOVE: the Pardoner
BELOW: Geoffrey Chaucer

old hand at pilgrimages, having 'done' Boulogne, Cologne, Compostela, Rome and Jerusalem. She tells of a knight who marries a 'loathly lady' in return for knowing what women most desire. The answer is 'sovereignty'; his reward is to see the old witch transformed into a young beauty.

More tales of marriage are told by the Oxford **Clerk**, an impoverished, poe-faced student; the elegant **Merchant**, who tells of an old husband and his unfaithful young wife; and the high-living **Franklin**, a lover of fish, flesh and 'alle deyntees that men koude thynke'.

Other tales, bawdy, romantic and moral, are told by the **Sergeant-at-Law**, learned and prudent yet always seeming 'bisier than he was'; the lusty, curly-haired **Squire**; the **Physician**, well grounded in surgery, astronomy and money-making (in league with apothecaries); the drunken, avaricious **Pardoner**, with his wallet full of pardons hot from Rome, who tells a moral tale about drunkenness and avarice; the ruthless, weather-beaten **Shipman**; the coy and affected **Prioress**; the worldly **Monk**, who loves 'a fat swan ... best of any roost'; the **Nun's Priest** and the **Second Nun**.

The **Canon's Yeoman** joins the travellers at Boughton-under-Blean with his sweating master, a fraudulent alchemist; the **Manciple**, who buys provisions for an inn of court, answers to 30 lawyers but makes fools of them all.

The final tale, the **Parson**'s, is a sermon on the Seven Deadly Sins, deploring the pride of current fashions, with short tunics revealing men's buttocks like 'the hyndre part of a she-ape in the fulle of the moone'.

ABOVE: the Cook

ABOVE: the Miller

OPPOSITE PAGE: the
cathedral pulpit

crude and extremely brutal life of his own times, but also the almost complete corruption of the Christian Church. That said, his lively and humorous text also reveals that these only too human people – obvious 'sinners' who enjoy all the sensuous pleasures of the flesh – are able to accept the spiritual into their lives with the same happy freedom as every other good gift.

himself to a life of simplicity and charity, and soon found himself at odds with the King about the disputed precedence of Court or Church in judging clergymen's misdemeanours.

The quarrel grew fierce and Becket fled to France, to be reconciled with Henry six years later in 1170. But they soon came into conflict once again. Henry, over in Normandy at

ABOVE: the scene of the crime: Canterbury Cathedral, where Thomas à Becket was martyred, inspiration for T S Eliot's play Murder in the Cathedral

BELOW: a Trinity Chapel window shows St Thomas appearing to William of Kellet in a dream

The history

Thomas à Becket was a complex character: friend of the King, ambitious, loved by the people, an archbishop slain on the altar-steps of his own cathedral by four armed knights. Born in Cheapside, London in 1118 of well-to-do Norman parents, he became the royal chancellor in 1155, serving Henry II for seven years as adviser, politician and soldier. In 1162 Henry appointed Thomas (who had studied canon law and taken deacon's orders) Archbishop of Canterbury, and was absolutely confounded to see his previously worldly and extravagant friend take up his ecclesiastic duties with a new fervour. Thomas devoted

the time, fell into a terrible fury, calling for someone to rid him of 'this turbulent priest'. Unfortunately, four of his knights took him at his word; they rushed across the Channel and hacked Thomas to death as he was praying in a side chapel in Canterbury Cathedral. This barbaric incident caused widespread horror throughout Christendom. Becket was immediately acclaimed as a martyr; Pope Alexander III canonised him in 1173 and Henry did public penance in his grief (and to appease his angry subjects).

The prudent collection of Becket's relics started immediately. 'While the body lay still on the pavement', wrote Brother Benedict, who claimed to have been near by at the time, 'some of the townsfolk of Canterbury brought bottles and carried off secretly as much of the blood as they could. Others cut shreds of clothing and dipped them into the blood.' And the blood left over 'was carefully and cleanly collected' by the monks, and 'poured into a clean vessel to be treasured up in the cathedral' – along with 'splinters of the sword which struck him down.'

Benedict gives the usual sickening details: 'When his monks stripped his body for burial they found him wearing drawers and a shirt both made of harsh knotted haircloth, swarming with vermin' (these lice were commonly known as the Pearls of Heaven). 'Indeed', according to one witness, 'so infested were they that anybody would judge the martyrdom light in comparison to wearing them'.

These garments were at once put on view in demonstration of Becket's 'heroic sanctity' and, as though further proof of his sufferings were needed, his emaciated body bore the severe lacerations of recent self-scourgings.

The miracles started that very night: a man smeared his paralysed wife with a scrap of cloth soaked in the blood, and she was cured. Twenty more cures were claimed in the next three weeks. A year later the pilgrims were flocking to the crypt in their droves and touching the coffin through the two holes in the tomb which the monks had made for this purpose when they built the shrine around it. Over the years, thousands more miracles were reported – mostly cures – and two monks were employed full-time keeping records of them.

There was soon a brisk export business in the cleanly collected blood, as phials of 'Canterbury Water' were distributed all over Europe: water to which drops of the martyr's blood were said to have been added – and continually diluted to meet the ever-growing public demand.

After his canonisation, Thomas's body eventually had to be moved from the crypt to a new chapel behind the high altar to make room for the vast crowds of pilgrims. There were all the usual mortifications of the flesh associated with his shrine, and pilgrims were expected to walk around it in bare feet or crawl along on their knees, with many paying the attendant monks to flog them as penance

RIGHT: a detail on the crypt, where St Thomas was originally buried

for their sins. His shrine became the focal point of the whole cathedral; even the sensible Erasmus was impressed: 'Every part glistened and shone and sparkled with rare and very large jewels, some of them bigger than the egg of a goose' (*Colloquy on Pilgrimage*).

A Venetian ambassador, accustomed to magnificence, described it more specifically: 'It surpasses all belief, because, notwithstanding the great size, it is entirely covered over with plates of pure gold, though the gold is scarcely visible from the variety of precious stones with which it is studded, as diamonds, emeralds, sapphires … But everything is left behind by a ruby given by the King of France' (*Medieval Pilgrims*, Alan Kendall).

BELOW: Canterbury today remains a magnet for pilgrims and tourists alike

During the Protestant Reformation of the 16th century, when Canterbury Cathedral was looted, it took six or seven strong men to lift the two enormous chests in which the jewels and precious metals of the shrine were to be carried to London – and 26 carts for all the other cathedral treasures.

Henry VIII, who was now the supreme head of the Church of England, had that great glowing ruby, the size of an apricot, mounted on a thumb-ring for himself.

Canterbury today

All that is left of such glories is an inscription on the wall near the place where Thomas was slain, the mosaic floor where his shrine stood and the worn stones of the pilgrims' steps leading to the chapel, speaking so eloquently of the human suffering and eternal hopes which they brought along with them. These stones, eroded over the centuries by countless pilgrims, are worth more than all the gold and jewels which once bedecked the shrine.

In the Middle Ages untold thousands of pilgrims walked on their own aching feet, or rode on horseback, and sometimes their journey took a year or more. The fervent would walk barefoot, and many would lower themselves to their knees for the last painful stretch. They would usually travel in company to protect themselves from the thieves lying in wait for easy pickings – though they could do little about the prices charged at the pilgrim hostels and inns.

Today, only the essential features of a pilgrimage remain: the journey itself, the holy destination and the travellers' shared purpose.

WALSINGHAM

For 500 years Walsingham drew pilgrims from all over Britain and beyond, to see the holy house built, it was said, according to the Virgin Mary's instructions. Today the site is once more the focus of Christian reverence and worship.

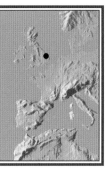

THE PILGRIMAGE to the Marian shrine at Walsingham, in north Norfolk, began just before the Norman conquest of 1066. By the time Thomas à Becket (see pages 108–14) was engaged in his battle of wills with Henry II, this was already a thriving religious centre.

The history

Lady Richeldis de Faverches, the rich widow of the local lord of the manor, had prayed to the Virgin Mary to tell her how she could best be honoured, and was granted a vision in which Mary took her in spirit to Nazareth and commanded her to build a replica of the holy house in which Jesus lived as a boy. Two springs of water appeared where the vision was seen, and that was taken as validation of the vision.

There were already several such holy houses in medieval Europe, the most famous enshrined in the basilica at Loreto, near Ancona in Italy, which was claimed to have been transplanted by the hands of angels from Nazareth (see pages 42–4).

However, this did not discourage the widow, who was given exact measurements and minute instructions, and a wooden hut was built which was significantly smaller than the stone house at Loreto. Then the Virgin, aided by angelic ministers, moved it 200 feet to its proper place and the pilgrims started arriving, encouraged to believe that

ABOVE: directing the pilgrims at Walsingham

BELOW: remains of the priory that welcomed medieval pilgrims

ABOVE: carrying the cross along the 'holy mile' to Walsingham in Easter week

BELOW: the Roman Catholic Shrine of Our Lady

this was the real thing: England's Nazareth.

The original hut was eventually surrounded by a thatched building of stone and flint. Then there was a large 11th-century priory for the Augustinian monks who were the guardians of the holy house, and then another priory was built in the 13th century, from which the Franciscan monks could provide welcome and hospitality to the ever-increasing number of pilgrims.

As at all such shrines, there were many valuable relics: a piece of the True Cross, some of the Virgin Mary's milk and a finger of St Peter, which could be kissed for a fee. But pride of place in the holy house was given to a wooden statue of the Virgin Mary seated with the child Jesus on her lap.

'Many sick been here cured', states a contemporary account of the signs and wonders which followed: 'Lame made hole and Blynde restored to syghte, the Dede agayne revyved … Lepers here recovered have be …'

There was all the usual commercial exploitation associated with such holy places, now as well as then; the more popular the shrine, the more pilgrims were attracted with what little wealth they had. No fewer than 17

inns were on hand to welcome the pilgrims, and the innkeepers earned a reputation for gross overcharging. They were not alone: the monks looked on their shrine as a source of income, led less than virtuous lives and did what they pleased with the money and jewels received.

The shrine was looted and destroyed during the Protestant Reformation of the 16th century, the statue of Our Lady of Walsingham was burned and the pilgrimage was largely forgotten, except by the faithful few who still came to pay their devotions here.

Walsingham today

At the beginning of this century the shrine was restored on a different site by an enthusiastic vicar of the Church of England. The Roman Catholics were not to be outdone, and there are now two shrines, neither on the known site of the original: the Church of England version in the village, and the Roman Catholic National Shrine of Our Lady about a kilometre or so out in the country. There is, however, a great deal of ecumenical

cooperation between them, especially shared pilgrimages on the feast days of the Virgin.

The Anglican shrine is housed in a small, modern brick church, with the holy house in an enclosed chapel, the heart and centre of which is a contemporary version of the original wooden statue, set high on an ornate altar. Mary wears a cross of jewel-encrusted gold, is dressed in gorgeous embroidered vestments, sits on a majestic throne and holds the child Jesus on her knees. In storage there is another crown, kept for use on various ceremonial occasions, and a wardrobe of equally gorgeous dresses.

Close by, in the sanctuary, there are three fragments of the True Cross and a number of other holy relics, and a holy well, the water of which pilgrims may drink as an aid to their spiritual healing. It is admitted that this well is not the same one used for a similar purpose in the Middle Ages, but the belief is that the water may possibly come from the same source – and three dowsers have apparently traced it in that direction.

The Roman Catholic shrine is a large and impressive contemporary wooden church, with a small separate chapel converted from the Saxon barn at which medieval pilgrims were supposed to have removed their shoes and made their confessions before walking barefoot into Walsingham (hence its present name, the Slipper Chapel). In it there is a wooden copy of the Anglican statue, though simpler and lacking the vestments.

The north Norfolk countryside has a clear light and serene beauty all its own, and many come on their own personal pilgrimages to Walsingham at all times of the liturgical year. There are also special ecumenical occasions on the feast days of the Virgin that feature (weather permitting) sung High Mass in the open air and candle-lit processions along the narrow streets of the village in the evening.

However, the main pilgrimage is at the end of Lent during Holy Week, when groups walk there from all over the country, each bringing a large wooden cross which members take turns to carry, their arrival timed for the afternoon of Good Friday. The groups of travellers then assemble into a formal procession to walk the last few kilometres into the village, many of them barefoot, and it is a most moving experience to hear them singing ancient pilgrim hymns as they come along the lane between the green hedges.

For the resurrection of Easter Sunday morning, the various crosses, now triumphant, are dressed in flowers and budding branches and coloured ribbons – a lovely ceremony, which has as much to do with the old pagan religion of Norfolk as it does with Christianity.

LEFT: the remains of a well in the priory ruins

BELOW: the Slipper Chapel

THE IMPORTANCE of the great mother goddess of prehistoric Europe is still apparent in these remote Norfolk landscapes. For example, a few kilometres to the south of Walsingham are the Neolithic flint-mines known as Grimes Graves, where archaeologists have found a propitiatory shrine on which the goddess was carved in chalk as a heavily pregnant woman.

GLASTONBURY

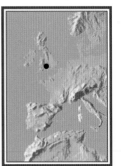

GLASTONBURY, in Somerset, is a holy place where the pagan and Christian worlds intersect and the New Age gathers. Christian pilgrims are drawn here by the tradition that Jesus visited these parts as a boy, again as a young man, and spent some time here in retirement before beginning his ministry in the Holy Land. Other visitors are attracted by the legends and mysteries of Arthurian Britain, and come to pay homage to the area's ancient Celtic past.

The history

The area around Glastonbury was once a wide smudge of brackish marshland and sandbanks, with the swamps and shallows extending in from the coast, broken here and there by low hummocks of mud and fringed by willows and yews, oaks and elms. Glastonbury Tor, the strange, almost pointed dome of a hill which dominates the landscape, was then an island in enchanted Avalon, the Celtic Land of the Dead, where King Arthur was taken after his last battle by the four weeping queens to be healed of his wound.

During the 12th century, bones believed by many to be those of King Arthur were discovered in an oak coffin, buried deep beneath the nave of the abbey.

The tradition that Jesus lived at Glastonbury is garnered from all over Somerset, Cornwall, the east of Ireland, and the south of France. It seems that Joseph of Arimathea, in whose own new rock tomb the dead Christ had been laid, was a younger brother of Mary's father, Joachim. He was also an importer of tin, lead and copper, which then flourished between Cornwall and Phoenicia; Britain was known as the Cassiterides, or the Islands of Tin. (Incidentally, in the even more distant past, this tin had supplied some of the glorious adornment of King Solomon's Temple in Jerusalem.)

On one of his voyages in a ship of Tarshish (modern Cadiz, in Spain), Joseph brought the boy Jesus with him. In gratitude for this adventure, the story goes, Jesus revealed to his great-uncle the secrets of purging tin from tungsten, and the pair of them stayed in various parts of Cornwall and Somerset, or 'Summer Land'.

About 15 or 20 years later, having appreciated the natural beauty and quiet peace of the area, Jesus returned on his own and settled in Glastonbury. He 'built with his own hands a small hermitage of mud and wattle, and spent some time in study, prayer and meditation. One possible source for this account is provided by St Augustine, who wrote to Pope Gregory the Great about the first followers of Christ coming to England and finding a church constructed by no human art, but by the hands of Christ himself.

During his time here Jesus preached, contacted the Druids and sowed the seeds for the future Christian Church in England.

After Joseph of Arimathea had buried Jesus in his rock tomb, he left Palestine to escape the persecution which resulted in Stephen's death by stoning and, with 11 disciples, set out for the same place of retreat. They were received by the local king, Aviragis, who granted them some land, and Joseph consecrated the little house of mud and wattle as a private chapel. This was later clad in

BELOW: New-Age travellers gather to celebrate at the chalk man of Glastonbury

LEFT: King Arthur and the Knights of the Round Table

wood for protection, and became the first church in Britain, always known as the Ealde Chiche or Old Church. In it Joseph placed a wooden carving of the Virgin Mary and water sprang from the hillside near by, and was believed to heal the sick.

Joseph had brought with him from Palestine two holy cruets containing some of the blood and sweat of the crucified Christ, and these were buried with him in the Old Church. The original cup of the Last Supper, usually called the Holy Grail, which Joseph had bought from the keeper of the inn where the first holy communion took place, is still said to be concealed where Joseph hid it.

That is by no means all of the Christian legend of Glastonbury. The Virgin Mary was also said to have travelled there in order to escape from Jewish and Roman persecution, and lived in Our Lady's Dowry, the same little house built by Jesus at Avalon. She was even said to have died in Britain and to have been laid to rest there in about AD 48.

According to the tale, Mary Magdalene and the two sisters of Bethany lived with the Virgin Mary, and the Madonna's beauty and rich singing voice endeared her to the local people, who venerated her as a saint even before she died. The main road through Glastonbury today is called Magdalene Street.

Other early Christians were said to have come to live in the area, too: Lazarus, the man whom Jesus had raised from the dead; Mary Salome and Mary Cleophas, two of the women who had witnessed the death of Christ on the cross, and who lived here with a black servant girl, Sara (who subsequently became the patron saint of thieves and gypsies); James the Just, a close relative of Jesus; Barnabas; Zaccheus and Luke. Finally, legend

BELOW: a shrine to Our Lady of Glastonbury

has it that the bodies of Peter and Paul were also brought to England to be buried.

Of course, legends are not records of facts; but the fascination with such legends is at least one reason why we go on pilgrimages.

Glastonbury today

There is still an annual Roman Catholic pilgrimage to the shrine of Our Lady, based on the likeness of her carved by Joseph of Arimathea. By the end of the 7th century the remains of the small house of mud and wattle had become the Wattle Church, which possessed a very ancient wooden statue of Our Lady (the implication being that it was the actual carving). This Wattle Church was eventually incorporated into the beginnings of what was to become a large Benedictine abbey. In the early 12th century, the whole of the abbey, including the Wattle Church, was burned and destroyed – though the statue itself survived. Two years after the disaster, a beautiful Romanesque Lady Chapel was built on the same site, and the statue was restored to its former position of glory.

Later still, a crypt was excavated to form a shrine in honour of St Joseph of Arimathea, and another chapel was erected near by, which re-created, as far as possible, the holy house of Our Lady at Loreto – probably in rivalry to the one at Walsingham.

The abbey was looted and destroyed during the Protestant Reformation, and its buildings soon became a stone quarry for the entire neighbourhood, though there is no record of what happened to the statue. But such was the reverence for the Lady Chapel that nobody would take part in its demolition, and this is now the most complete part of existing remains.

In 1955 a new statue of Our Lady of Glastonbury was blessed and restored to the ancient shrine; 10 years later it was crowned and High Mass was sung in the abbey ruins. Pilgrims continue to come here on Mary's major feast days.

Perhaps the largest and happiest of all pilgrimages to Glastonbury these days, however, are those of the emerging New-Age Folk. Their festivals, celebrations, conferences, workshops and guided tours are all based on the idea that the spirit of pilgrimage can rejuvenate physically and spiritually, offering an alternative to our present way of life. To this end, visitors tread the Cretan Spiral Maze up Glastonbury Tor, see the terrestrial zodiac set out in the fields and contours of the surrounding landscape and learn about its mystical relationship to the Arthurian Cycle, visit Chalice Hill Well, in which the Holy Grail has apparently been hidden, talk about Druids and Celtic mythology, eat, drink, sing and dance in celebration of human life and love.

ABOVE: banners and processions celebrate the annual Catholic pilgrimage to Glastonbury

MAIN PICTURE: the familiar sight of Glastonbury Tor
LEFT: pilgrims of another persuasion – New-Age visitors to Glastonbury pitch their tents and prepare for a festival of their own

I O N A

On a tiny island in the Hebrides, off the shores of Mull, a Christian settlement was founded that was to become the 'cradle of Christianity' for 6th-century Scots. With its tranquil setting and turbulent past, Iona can still cast a spell.

OPPOSITE PAGE: the abbey overlooking the sea on Iona

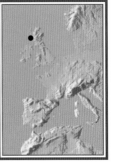

THE GREEN TURF and worn stones of Iona, one of the smaller islands of the Inner Hebrides, off the stormy west coast of Scotland by the Ross of Mull, were holy long before St Columba made this a focus of Christianity in northern Britain. There is evidence that the sun was worshipped on Iona, and a great stone slab outside the door of St Oran's Chapel is a legacy of those days. At one time there was a white marble stone in each of the three smooth hollows in its surface, and every visitor had to turn the three stones round three times in the direction of the sun. If they did not, the Last Trump would sound, and the Day of Judgement would be upon them there and then. But when the stones had worn through the slab with all their turning, the world would end. So the only choice was between the fire and the trumpet.

The whole island has always had a rather mysterious quality that sets it apart and enhances its reputation as one of the great pilgrimages of the world.

The history

Iona's Christian tradition began in the 6th century with the arrival of Columba, son of Phelim, of the royal Irish house of Niall of the Nine Hostages. A contemporary account in the island's guide book describes him as 'a typical Irishman, vehement, irresistible ... hear him curse a niggardly rich man or bless the heifers of a poor peasant ... see him follow a robber, cursing the wretch to his destruction, after him to the water's edge, wading up to his knees in the clear green sea-water, with both hands raised to Heaven in imprecation'.

Born in Donegal in 521, Columba spent his early years studying, copying rare manuscripts, teaching, setting up churches and monasteries and fighting. He took part in the Battle of Cooldrevne, led, it was said, by the archangel Michael, losing only one man and slaying 3,000 of the pagan enemy. These activities prompted his excommunication by the Irish Church elders, but they relented and sent Columba to win as many souls for the Church as had been lost in the battle.

Eventually, at the age of 40, he picked 11 companions and set sail in the early summer of AD 563, heading north to the islands off the coast of western Scotland in a coracle made of a framework of slender branches covered by hides made taut with thongs of leather.

After six or seven days and nights they landed in a cove on the south coast of Iona, known to this day as Port of the Coracle, and Columba climbed the nearest hill to be sure that Ireland was out of sight; the hill is still known as The Hill with its Back to Ireland.

From then on, truth and legend are inextricably tangled in Columba's story. St Oran, one of the 11 companions, apparently offered to be buried alive as a sacrifice to make the place holy. So they dug him a grave to his size and chosen depth and buried him. After three

BELOW: St Columba depicted in stained glass

ABOVE: the surviving walls of the Iona nunnery
RIGHT: a decorated cross in the abbey grounds

days they opened the grave and found Oran alive and proclaiming that 'There is no such wonder in death, nor is Hell what it has been described'. So they buried him again.

There is nothing left now of the church which Columba and his followers built, except the foundations on the little hillock opposite the west door of the present small cathedral, the last remains of his cell and the naked rock floor on which he slept, with a pillow of stone. From the monastery which they founded here, with its beehive-shaped cells of timber and turf, refectory and guest house, Columba and the others set out to preach to the Picts (whose king, Bude, was converted) and to travel across Britain, founding more monasteries on the way.

Columba died on Iona in 597; his remains were exhumed a century later and given a shrine of silver and gold, bringing more pilgrims to pray before his bones. When the first of the Viking raiders arrived, plundering and murdering, the monks fled to the safety of Kells in Ireland, and the island was eventually left deserted.

Iona today

Iona is not quite as it was, but the pilgrims are still coming. In 1938 the Iona Community was set up by the Presbyterian Church to restore the buildings and offer spiritual retreat. The modern bronze sculpture of the Virgin Mary in the cloisters was made by Jacob Lipchitz, a devout Jew, who created it

BELOW: the Abbey of St Columba by candlelight

with the intention of gaining a better understanding among all peoples: a fitting addition to this beautiful and holy site. Two hundred thousand make the journey every year, presumably agreeing with Samuel Johnson's observation to James Boswell: 'That man is little to be envied whose piety would not grow warmer among the ruins of Iona.'

It may not be as easy to share in that pious atmosphere these days, yet there is still a timeless tranquillity here: wild flowers grow in the joints and crannies of the ruined church walls; weathered Celtic crosses and the ancient worn stones and tombs remain; and it is still possible to feel Columba's sense of wonder when he wrote: 'Delightful I think it to be in the bosom of the isle, on the peak of a rock, that I might often watch there the calm of the sea ... hear the sound of the shallow waves against the rocks ... the very noise of the sea ... its ebb and flood-tide in their flow ...'

Here, with the Ross of Mull across the water and the Bay of Martyrs, where the Vikings slaughtered 68 holy men, and the White Strand of the Monks, where the Norsemen slaughtered 16 more, it is still a moving experience to stand with the ocean before you, the white doves of the abbey swirling through the skies above and the bones of the ancient dead beneath your feet.

'In Iona of my heart', Columba had foretold, 'in Iona of my love, instead of the voices of monks shall be the lowing of cattle ... but, e'er the world comes to an end, Iona shall be as it was.'

LINDISFARNE

Off the east coast of the north of England, just south of the Scottish Borders and about a kilometre out to sea, is the Holy Island of Lindisfarne. As the tide ebbs and flows, the place is surrounded by the sea twice a day, and twice a day the sand dries into a causeway connecting it with the mainland.

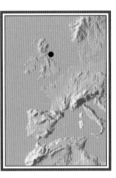

*L*IFE ON *LINDISFARNE* is dominated by the sea, so that its visitors have to time their arrival when the tide is out and ensure that they do not stay too long – or they must stay the night.

The history

Lindisfarne was first made holy in the 7th century by Aiden, a Scot from the community of monks on Iona (see pages 122–4): 'A bishop of wonderful gentleness, holiness, and moderation', wrote the Venerable Bede in his *History of the English Church and People*, 'much given to humility and poverty'.

King Oswald of Northumbria, 'a man beloved of God', according to Bede, 'granted the island to Aiden as a base for the conversion of the kingdom'. Aiden was a good man, for he loved to give alms to the poor whom he met on his travels (he always travelled everywhere on foot). Moreover, wrote Bede, 'if wealthy people did wrong, he never kept silent out of respect or fear'.

Although there is a great, gaunt bronze statue of Aiden in front of his beloved priory on Lindisfarne, he could not have lived many of his days there, for he was always travelling, preaching, seeking new ways of doing good,

cultivating peace and love, comforting the sick and protecting the poor. Not much of his work is left on the island: the first monastery was sacked by the Danes towards the end of the 8th century, and again in the middle of the 9th. 'From the wrath of the Northman,' was Aiden's prayer, 'O Lord, please protect us'.

The present ruins are those of the Benedictine priory that was built during the 11th century; according to legend, the masons and carpenters who erected it were supplied with their bread from the air and with their wine from an inexhaustible chalice. But the place was looted and destroyed by Thomas Cromwell's men during the Protestant Reformation of the 16th century, and the rain and sea-winds of centuries did the rest.

Lindisfarne today

There are still regular pilgrimages here, but considerable imagination is needed to walk with Aiden at all. Along the narrow concrete causeway that runs across at low tide, cars are bumper to bumper during the tourist season, competing for space with the ice-cream vans. Yet there are also the screaming gulls, spread-eagled against the wind, the wild flowers that

BELOW: the 11th-century priory ruins on Lindisfarne

TOP: the northern wall of Lindisfarne Castle, converted in the early-20th century by architect Sir Edwin Lutyens
ABOVE: Lutyens' Ship Room
BELOW: the remains of Lindisfarne Priory

grow here in profusion, the drenched grass, the grey-green sea lapping against the beach, the drifts of pebbles underfoot and, away to the south-east, the Farne Islands, the haunt of seals and seabirds.

The Lindisfarne Gospels, which are kept in the British Museum in London, are from the first monastery on the island, and were copied from the Latin of Jerome. Written and illuminated on vellum at the end of the 7th century, most of the text is plain calligraphy, some of the loveliest handwriting ever penned, with decorated initial capitals here and there like small jewels. But the main treasures are at the beginning of each gospel, where the whole page is covered with interlacing patterns of spirals and boughs, branches and birds, beasts, flowers and faces.

During a raid by the dreaded Northmen the Gospels were washed into the sea and lost – only to be rediscovered, intact and largely undamaged, stranded along the beach of a distant coast. This may be no more than a legend – but the pages of the Lindisfarne Gospels do bear the stains of seawater.

CUTHBERT WAS a monk of Lindisfarne who was called to his vocation on the very night Aiden died. Like Francis of Assisi, he was a friend of all living creatures, and used to have sea-otters gambolling at his feet when he was walking the shores, and the birds of the air feeding him. He craved solitude, and eventually dug himself a cell in the rocks of the Farne Islands, made a low wall around it and built a roof of thatch over it. His only companions were the seals and the gulls, and he lived there, according to Bede, 'in peace of mind'.

LATTER-DAY SAINTS

·

*The American Latter-Day Saints – or Mormons, as they are still popularly
known – have a relatively short history, but one which is marked by violence
and persecution on a horrifying scale. Their's is also one of the most
courageous journeys ever made for a religious goal.*

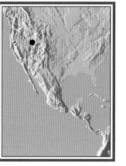

JOSEPH SMITH, founder of the Mormons, was born in 1805 in Sharon, Vermont. At the age of 14 he was so troubled by the rivalry of Baptists and Methodists that he retired to the woods in Manchester, New York, in prayer. Here God and Jesus Christ appeared to him. He questioned them both about which of the various denominations was right, and was told by God that all were wrong, all their creeds being 'an abomination in his sight'.

Three years later, Joseph Smith had another vision, repeated three times, in which a person appeared, 'glorious beyond description', who gave his name as Moroni, son of Mormon, and promised that a book written on golden plates would soon be entrusted to him for translation, along with two clear jewels in silver bows to act as spectacles by which to read the text.

Smith went to the place described by Moroni – a hill near Palmyra, New York – and found the golden plates and reading lenses in a stone box under a large rock. In his own words: 'The plates had the appearance of gold, six inches wide and eight inches long, and thin. They were filled with engravings, in Egyptian characters, and bound together in a

volume' (quoted in Salt Lake City's *History of the Church of Latter-Day Saints*). The two transparent stones were, Smith noted, obviously the Urim and Thummin, the oracular gems used by the High Priest of Israel to reveal the will of God to man. However, not until he was 22 was he eventually entrusted with the contents of the stone box (there being no very clear reason for the delay).

He at once began to copy the characters from the plates and, by wearing the spectacles as he had been instructed, to begin the arduous work of translation.

According to witnesses, Smith did this by two methods. One involved putting the seer stones into a hat, with one of the golden plates inside it, and then putting his face into the hat, drawing it closely around his face to exclude the light and reading the characters and their interpretation into the English of the Authorised Version of the Bible. A scribe would write the words down.

By the other method, Smith would place himself behind a curtain, look through the lenses at the plates, decipher the characters into English and hand copies from behind the curtain to those on the outside.

BELOW: Joseph Smith

The completed translation was published in 1830, and is known as the *Book of Mormon*, while the golden plates and spectacles were taken back on the day of publication and deposited by Moroni in their resting place – 'in the Heavenly Courts above'.

The story told in the Book of Mormon is complicated and often confusing. It is about two great waves of immigration to America from the Middle East, soon after the failure of the Tower of Babel (The Old Testament, Genesis XI: 1–9). One wave set sail in eight barges and, after being driven west by the wind for 344 days, landed on the Atlantic coast of Central America. The other built a ship under divine instruction, sailed east across the Indian and Pacific oceans and landed on the coast of what is now Peru. They built great cities and civilisations, though they all but destroyed themselves warring with one another, and their survivors were among the ancestors of the Native Americans, or Indians. All of this, and much more, is accepted by Mormons as gospel.

ABOVE: *Brigham Young, inheritor of the Mormon cause*

Joseph Smith founded the Church of Jesus Christ of Latter-Day Saints in Fayette, New York, in 1830, with six members; a month later he had won 40 souls to his congregation. Soon after this he began to compile an 'inspired revision' of the entire Bible; he claimed that previous editions had been translated incorrectly, or so rendered as to make the intended meaning obscure.

BELOW: *the Mountain Meadows Massacre, 1857*

Then another vision revealed to Smith that Independence, Missouri, was the Land of Promise, and the place for the City of Zion, so Smith and his followers sold up, left New England and settled there.

It is generally admitted by neutral contemporary observers that the Mormons were quiet, industrious and economical, honest and peaceful and that they displayed much skill, energy and enthusiasm. But the original settlers of Missouri resented the newcomers, especially when they referred to themselves as the 'new chosen people' – so their farms and homes came under brutal attack and the Mormon settlers were themselves run out of town.

Similar persecution happened everywhere they went. At Haun's Mill, Missouri, in 1838, the Governor ordered the General of Militia to treat the Mormons as enemies and to exterminate them or drive them from the state. Men, women and children were shot down as they fled to the woods. A certain Brother Merrick was cut to pieces with a corn-cutter, and a nine-year-old boy, Sardius Smith, was found hiding in terror and had the upper part of his head blown off by a soldier who used his rifle at point-blank range. The soldiers then proceeded to rob the Mormons' houses, waggons and tents of their bedding and clothing, drove off their horses and waggons, leaving the surviving widows and orphans destitute, and even stripped the bodies of their victims. The whole episode has been called one of the most shameful incidents of American domestic history.

MORMON archaeologists have claimed that both North and South America are rich in the remains of the Middle Eastern immigrants, their civilisation and their '38 great cities'. The Smithsonian Institute in Washington states, however, that 'there is no correspondence whatsoever between archaeological sites and cultures as revealed by scientific investigations, and as revealed in the Book of Mormon'.

Research workers at the Department of Anthropology at Columbia University have said that 'there is not a single fact of value concerning the prehistory of the American Indian in the Book of Mormon ... It is untrue biblically, historically and scientifically'.

Brigham Young University at Salt Lake City, the intellectual heartland of Mormonism, claims that its own research conclusions demonstrate that everybody else is absolutely wrong.

Other mobs looted and burned Mormon settlements elsewhere and Joseph Smith himself was tarred and feathered, imprisoned on various occasions, manacled in heavy chains and leg-irons, and his followers beaten or killed. In 1840 the movement made its new base in Illinois, calling its community Nauvoo and gathering 20,000 members.

Eventually, to prevent further persecution and shedding of blood, Smith surrendered himself to the Governor and was held in the local gaol at Carthage, Illinois, where, on 27 July 1844, when he was 39, he was lynched by an armed mob of 200 men and shot down with a volley of rifle-shots through the body. There was then an attempt to saw his head from his body with a knife.

The survivors were driven out of Nauvoo and Smith's successor as their president, Brigham Young, led most of them on the famous gruelling trek from Illinois to Salt Lake Valley in Utah, a land that nobody wanted – surely one of the most inspiring stories in the long history of the search for religious freedom: a true pilgrimage.

Four hundred waggons of would-be settlers – men, women and children – with a small herd of cattle and a few chickens in coops, set out to endure cold, hunger, exposure, thirst, hostile Native Americans and unfriendly settlements on their journey of well over 2,000km across the Great Plains. They continued through the steep passes up into the Rocky Mountains, hundreds dying on the way, and down into the bleak valley, to what is now Salt Lake City. Here, they made the desert blossom and were visited by various 'miracles' – such as their first harvest in 1848, saved when thousands of gulls appeared from Salt Lake and devoured a plague of locusts.

It is a sad fact, however, that the Mormons were themselves responsible for a number of barbaric acts. For example, in 1857 Brigham Young ordered the annihilation of a waggon train of 150 non-Mormon immigrants, in what became known as the Mountain Meadows Massacre – for which, 20 years later, those responsible were convicted and executed. Young had been appointed Governor of Utah Territory in 1850, but the growing practice of polygamy alarmed the US

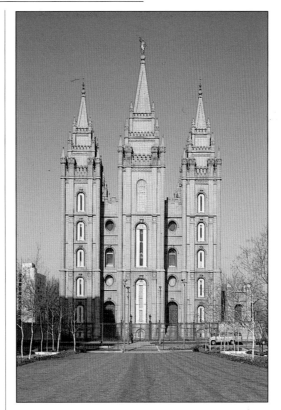

LEFT: the Mormon temple in Salt Lake City, Utah

Government and a non-Mormon governor was put in place in 1869. When Young died in 1877 he left 17 wives and 56 children.

The Mormons today

There are over 4 million Mormons today, most of whom live in the United States. Their headquarters are still in Salt Lake City, a temple to rival in size and importance the Shrine of the Immaculate Conception in Washington, and a history of hard work and achievement. It took exactly 40 years to build the temple, made of granite quarried 30km away and hauled to the site in ox carts; the building boasts six spires and a cast-copper statue of the angel Moroni raising his golden trumpet to his lips to herald the second coming of Christ.

Next door to the temple is the Tabernacle, with a huge, turtle-shaped roof: this holds 7,000 people and is equipped with an organ of 12,000 pipes and six keyboards. The famous Mormon Tabernacle Choir is more than 200 strong, and has made several recordings. All a far cry from the days of rejection and persecution; and a far cry from the vision and meditation of the young Joseph Smith.

ISLAM

T HE NAME OF MECCA has become synonymous with pilgrimage far
beyond the Muslim world, but only followers of Islam may enter their
holiest of cities, the birthplace of Muhammad. All Muslims are expected to
make a pilgrimage to Mecca at least once, and wherever they are in the world,
they face Mecca when they pray.

Muslims from all over the world are drawn to Mecca in their thousands

MECCA

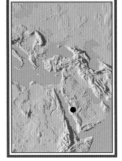

ABOVE: *an illustration of the mosque at Mecca, from a Persian text by Mustafa Al-Shukri*

*F*ROM *MECCA* (Makkah) and its surrounding granite peaks, barren and vaguely hostile, the level sands of Saudi Arabia stretch away, punctuated with thorn-bushes and scrub and scorched by the sun. A few kilometres to the west is the world's largest airport, open for only six weeks of the year (the dates vary), with 12 enormous terminals and a jumbo jet landing every five minutes, bringing in 4,000 people an hour for these crowded days. A concrete and asphalt freeway called the Corridor of Dedication cuts through the mountains. At the exit from the freeway, a sign reads: 'Stop for inspection now. Entry prohibited to non-Muslims.' This is the holy ground of Mecca, the biggest pilgrimage of them all.

The history

Muhammad was born in Mecca towards the end of the 6th century. His father, a poor merchant belonging to the Quaraysh tribe, died before his birth; his mother died when he was only six years old, and Muhammad was brought up by his grandfather and uncle. Very little is known for certain about his upbringing: he was trained to be a merchant, lived in the tents of the nomads, travelled to Syria and met holy men. It is apparent that he emerged dissatisfied with the polytheism and superstitions of his own people, and critical of both Judaism and Christianity.

At the age of 25, now a trader, Muhammad married a wealthy widow 15 years older than himself, Khadija. Their life together was extremely happy, and they had six children. Again, little is known about him during the

OPPOSITE PAGE: *Muslims at the Ka'ba, the House of Allah*

15 years before his call by Allah.

It is said that Muhammad passed through what Christians would regard as the dark night of the soul: spiritual exhaustion, even doubt; and that it was his custom to retire to mountain caves to give himself up to fasting, prayer and meditation. In about 610 he was granted the gift of ecstatic utterance, and at the age of 40 or 42 he was called by Allah to be a prophet with one message: 'the almighty power of the One Almighty, and man's duty of obedience'. Allah's commands were expressed over the coming years in the words of the Qur'an (or 'reading'), as revealed to Muhammad from the writings on tablets kept in the courts of Paradise. The Prophet's preaching about One Almighty God led to inevitable trouble with the religious authorities at Mecca, who were in charge of a long venerated and profitable sanctuary of their many gods – guarded by Muhammad's own tribe, the Quaraysh. If Muhammad succeeded in converting the people to the worship of Allah, the sanctuary would cease to be of any use. Ironically, this sanctuary, the Ka'ba, was later to become the House of Allah and the centre of Islamic pilgrimage.

After the death of Khadija, in the face of accusations of sorcery, charges of fraud and other attacks, Muhammad was ultimately

I*N THE COURSE* of the 'holy war', terrible atrocities were committed in Allah's name. For example, 800 captured Jews were made to dig a mass grave, forced to kneel at its edge and beheaded in one day and night, while their women and children watched before being sold into concubinage and slavery. Only one Jew saved his life by renouncing Jehovah.

RIGHT: the faithful at prayer outside al-Harram Mosque, home of the Ka'ba

ABOVE: Muslims gather for Hajj, the annual journey to Mecca demanded by Muhammad and made in the Islamic lunar month of Dhu-ul-Hijja

forced to flee to Medina (Al Madinah; see pages 136–7), 300km to the north, where he already had followers. His journey there, in 622, is known as the Hagira, and marks the dawning of the Muhammadan Era.

Muhammad usually displayed tact and diplomacy in his dealings with others, but though he was sure that his message was for all Arabs, even all mankind, he quickly decided that people could only be convinced by force, and that there could be no compromise with idolatry. He was capable of winning support by eloquence and persuasion but, when that failed, he could be ruthless. So, like the Jews and Christians before him, Muhammad took to the sword and those who would not accept Islam were faced with death.

First, he expelled Jews from the territory which he controlled, then he preached war against the infidels as a sacred duty, or *jihad*. By 629, after a series of brilliantly planned and courageously led battles, Muhammad was master of Mecca. Within another year he had taken control of all Arabia.

Muhammad entered Mecca in triumph, smashed the 350 idols which surrounded the Ka'ba, and is supposed to have 'cleaned' off paintings of Jesus from its walls, while preserving those of Mary, before establishing the sanctuary as the centre of pilgrimage for all Islam. He died in 632, soon after returning from his last journey to Mecca. By the time of

his death, Muhammad had shaped the Arab world for centuries to come: less than a hundred years after his death the Muslim empire stretched from southern France through Spain, North Africa, the Levant and Central Asia to the Great Wall of China.

Mecca today

The most important ritual and moral duties incumbent on all Muslims are called the Five Pillars: declaration of belief in the One True and living God; prayer at least five times a day; giving of alms to the poor; fasting; and pilgrimage to Mecca.

The declaration of belief, or the creed, is the shortest of any faith: 'There is no God but God, and Muhammad is the prophet of God.' Prayer is more complicated, and involves a strictly prescribed ritual of stances, bowings and prostrations while facing Mecca, with the words to be said in Arabic while in a state of bodily purity. Fasting is mostly concentrated during Ramadan, the ninth month of the Muslim year, when all true believers except the sick, travellers, pregnant women, nursing mothers and young children are required to abstain from all food, drink, smoking and sexual intercourse from dawn until sunset. The giving of alms to the poor is said to bring God's blessing for every beggar who receives charity. The pilgrimage to Mecca is required of every adult Muslim, man or woman, at least once in a lifetime, if they can afford it.

Mecca was a place of pilgrimage long before Islam: the Qur'an says that Abraham, Father of Israel, started the custom, and it is said that his son, Ishmael, Father of the Arab people, laid the paved area of green serpentine stone on which the Ka'ba was built.

The Ka'ba began as the sanctuary of many gods: a large, rough cube of grey-green granite blocks, slightly longer than a perfect square, with one diagonal aligned north to south, the other more or less east to west, obviously with some early astronomical significance.

At one corner is set a large black stone, supposedly a meteorite, set there by Muhammad himself. When floods weakened the foundations of the Ka'ba, four groups of workmen from four different tribes were appointed to rebuild it, each group responsible for one wall. When it came to the honour of resetting the black stone there was trouble; a fight broke out, oaths were taken and blood was spilled. Then the prophet suggested that one man from each group should hold the stone between them on a cloth, one at each corner, while he guided it into position.

The main purpose of the contemporary Muslim pilgrimage to Mecca is to circle the Ka'ba seven times anticlockwise, and to touch and kiss the black stone. At one time, it is said, the pilgrims did this naked, as an expression of holy innocence, but now they are expected to wear the white *ihram*, two regulation lengths of cloth, one from the waist to

the shins, usually held up by tucking, the other loose over the shoulders. The tradition is the pilgrims should take their *ihram* back home with them for use as a shroud.

Mecca itself resembles a Hollywood film set for a cinema epic. Five-star hotels, expensive shops and gas-guzzling automobiles are now part of the landscape, though most of it is as timeless as the pilgrimage: bazaars, alleys, food stalls and little secluded courtyards.

Al-Harram, or the sacred precinct, in which the Ka'ba rests, is the largest open-air temple in the world, where between 1 and 2 million people gather every year to worship. Teeming crowds mill around, all with one purpose: to enter the place by the Gate of Peace, to take off their sandals, to step across the threshold right foot first, to move slowly along pavements, around galleries and curving halls, between slender pillars, down aisles past families sitting cross-legged, resting or reading the Qur'an, over marble courtyards and through arcades towards the Ka'ba at the heart of the central courtyard. There is no rushing and hardly any pushing or shoving; men and women cry with relief or joy, look around in wonder, repeat words from the Qur'an and pray, moving on in the steady stream towards the Ka'ba, the one still point in all this activity, beneath its black curtain. Around it sway the pilgrims, always to the right, circling 10 or 20 deep: thousands of men and women, calling out the ritual prayer at the corners – a different call at every one, and a special prayer at the black stone – until seven circuits have been completed.

ABOVE: pilgrims have their hair cut off in preparation for their holy journey

LEFT: kissing the holy stone, set at one corner of the Ka'ba by Muhammad

MEDINA

'Medina,' Muhammad once said, 'was to me the cradle of Moses on the Nile.'

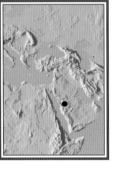

THE CITY OF MEDINA (Al Madinah) is the second most venerated place of pilgrimage for devout Muslims, largely because it is where the Prophet Muhammad is buried, but also because of its importance in the history of Islam – for this is where he conducted his military campaign to overcome the long resistance of Mecca to his religious teachings.

The history

After coming into conflict with the guardians of the sanctuary in Mecca, where many gods were worshipped (see pages 132–5), Muhammad had to flee for his life. Several neighbouring towns rejected him, and even stoned him to drive him away. But he was allowed to enter Yathrib, an oasis lying to the north of Mecca.

Founded by the Jews at the intersection of three ancient caravan routes, Yathrib was the commercial centre of a productive date-growing

Egyptian Muslims offer up their prayers at their journey's end in Medina

area, an important market for gold, and a place where many Christians felt safe enough to live. Muhammad soon established himself there, and Yathrib subsequently became known as Madinat-un-nabi, or 'City of the Prophet' – Medina, as it is called today.

Muhammad lived there for a few years, refined his teachings and grew in power and influence. Finally, in an attempt to convert by the sword, he organised a series of raids on caravans and surrounding towns, including Mecca, still the heart of his spiritual world. An army of over 10,000 men was raised against his little band of around 400 disciples and followers, but Muhammad was a master of desert warfare and fortified Medina, refusing to be drawn into a fight except on his choice of ground. Slowly, he wore his enemies down, until they were ready to sign a truce. He then subjugated Mecca, destroyed the idols around the Ka'ba and made it the centre of Islamic pilgrimage.

The first mosque, or place of prayer, at Medina was extremely simple. A square of ground was enclosed by a wall of sun-dried bricks; there were palm trees to provide the very necessary shade, and about a third of this area was thatched over with palm leaves. Then three doorways were opened in the walls: one facing Jerusalem, one for Jibril to enter, and one called the Gate of Mercy. The courtyard was used for prayer and as a place of shelter for the homeless, thus combining the two most essential aspects of Islamic practice: praise and compassion in the name of Allah.

From the simplicity of this first mosque there developed the complex beauty of some of the world's most inspiring religious buildings, wonders of marble and gold.

Medina today

The journey to Medina is usually made as a pious addition to the pilgrimage to Mecca, either before it – to 'get to know' the Prophet – or afterwards, to seal his message. Indeed Muhammad is reported as having said that anyone going on pilgrimage to Mecca without visiting his tomb would be churlish. This is not a formal religious requirement, but most pilgrims make the effort, travelling the 300km of desert from Mecca by road or air.

Medina is a typical modern Arab city of low white buildings, with palm trees lining the streets and six-lane highways running in several directions. Unlike Mecca, it has fruitful earth and lush vegetation, and the air is fresh. The mosque is not as large as that in Mecca, but it has its own powerful presence: rose-pink granite, decorated with tiles and mosaics, pierced screens and gold. At its heart is a small enclosure where Muhammad lived and taught, the mud-brick house where he ate and slept and the tomb where he is buried.

BELOW: sunset over the glorious mosque at Medina

SIKHISM

SIKHISM WAS FOUNDED in the 15th century by Guru Nanak, who promoted the quest for inner truth above any outward show of ritual or formality. He was first in a line of ten gurus (the last died in 1708), whose teachings form the sacred book known as Guru Granth Sahib. The oldest copy of the scriptures is in the Golden Temple at Amritsar, which every Sikh will try to visit once in a lifetime.

Part temple, part mosque, the Golden Temple at Amritsar has been the focus of passionate battles

THE GOLDEN TEMPLE

ABOVE: the Golden
Temple of Amritsar

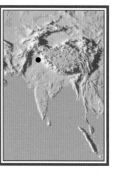

BELOW: Gobind Singh,
founder of the Khalsa

*T*HE VARIOUS Islamic incursions into India between the 7th and 12th centuries destroyed much of the ancient religious culture of the north, but left the less accessible south comparatively unchanged. In the Punjab, even across the border into Kashmir, there arose a genuine blend of Hindu devotion and elements of Islam.

In the early-15th century, an Islamic weaver called Kabir became the disciple of a Hindu guru, Ramanand, and from their work together the teaching known as the Kabirpanth developed: 'O God, whether Allah or Vishnu, I live by your holy name.' Many years later, a Hindu of Lahore – Guru Nanak (1469–1539) – came under the influence of the Kabirpanth and founded a new religious and political movement: Sikhism. Today, though still centred in the Punjab, Sikhs are to be found all over India and the Far East, with significant settlements in Britain.

The history of Sikhism

Guru Nanak believed that the worship of God was hindered by ritual and encouraged meditation and private devotion instead. He was, according to Sikh belief, one of a line of 10 gurus to bring the word of God to humanity. The last of this line, Guru Gobind Singh (1666–1708) came to prominence at a time of fierce conflict between the Sikhs and the ruling Mughal empire. Under Gobind Singh's leadership Sikhs became skilled warriors. He introduced the Khalsa, the Sikh community, whose members wore the 'five Ks': Kes (uncut hair); Kangha (a comb); Kirpan (a dagger); Kara (a bracelet), and Kachh (shorts). All men were called Singh ('lion') and women Kaur ('princess').

After Guru Gobind Singh the notion of a guru was transferred to the holy scripture, Adi Granth, which contains the sayings of Nanak and his successors. From then on the sacred book was known as Guru Granth Sahib.

Sikhism today

Sikh beliefs are simple, though with profound implications. God is beyond any human comprehension – yet is the one and only reality; everything else is illusion. This God is known by many names, all of them holy, and the best way of approach is through the ritual repetition of these holy names, singing hymns of praise and meditation under the personal guidance of a guru or teacher.

Magnificent hand-written and decorated copies of the Guru Granth Sahib are treasured in every Sikh place of worship, the oldest being at their Golden Temple at Amritsar, the City of Immortality. The scriptures are treated with meticulous reverence, and may only be touched by a Sikh. The book is usually wrapped in a cloth of embroidered silk and kept in a box of carved cedar or sandalwood. On high festivals the scriptures are recited aloud from cover to cover by relays of readers, a process which requires at least two full days.

The Golden Temple, or Harimandir, is a noble and strangely beautiful building: part temple, part mosque and marked by time and the passionate battles which have recently been fought between Sikhs and Hindus for its possession. Built in 1766, it stands on a holy lake and is decorated with copper-gilt inscriptions from the scriptures.

Because Sikhs are currently demanding political independence and the establishment of a separate state, thousands of them have been imprisoned by the Indian government. There have been incidents of terrorism perpetrated by both sides, and several times the Indian army has launched assaults on Sikh militants occupying the Golden Temple – battles fought with extreme bitterness. The walls have been blackened with flames, raked by machine-guns, pitted by grenades and

LEFT: a Sikh takes his turn to recite verses from the Guru Granth Sahib

mortars. Its windows have been shattered and strands of rusting barbed wire are still tangled across the temple gates. But despite all this violence the Golden Temple survives, and is being repaired, even partially rebuilt.

No matter how many battles rage around and inside it, the temple remains, like the Ka'ba at Mecca, a true holy place, sacred to all believers. Pilgrimage is not specifically required, though most Sikhs go there at least once in their lives – but non-believing tourists have never been encouraged. With separatist violence still smouldering and likely to flare at any moment, the Golden Temple at Amritsar should be left to its worshippers.

BELOW: a highly colourful Sikh ceremony

HINDUISM

HINDUISM IS A RELIGION of great diversity, with many gods and many variations in the form of worship. Holy places are all within the Indian sub-continent, but they number in tens of thousands. The major places of pilgrimage are those associated with Shiva, Krishna and Vishnu – and the River Ganges, believed to purify all who enter its waters.

The faithful crowd into the bathing ghats at Varanasi, India

HINDU FAITH

A Hindu pilgrim meditates to prepare for the arduous journey ahead of him

*T*WO HINDU men, wearing long, not very clean white robes and loose turbans, are sweeping the centre of the road barefoot, with street-sweeper brooms. Both are low-caste, both are chanting. They are preparing the way for a holy man on pilgrimage to a temple of Shiva. He is naked except for a voluminous loin-cloth and his head is shaved; a red line is painted down the middle of his forehead, a white line on either side. His body is thin, but with sharply defined muscles and tendons, and he makes slow progress. He stands, says 'Shiva', kneels, prays aloud, prostrates himself full-length, prays aloud again, kneels, says 'Shiva', scrabbles forward on his knees to where his head had been during his prostration, gets to his feet and begins the process again. His two disciples sweep aside the dust and small stones, while another disciple, behind him, collects alms in a wooden bowl. It will probably take the holy man a week to travel the 10km to Shiva's temple. A deeply ridged callous marks each knee: he has been crawling on them for months.

Other holy men make their pilgrimage all the way on their knees, along tens or hundreds of kilometres, month after month, towards Brahma or Shiva or Vishnu. Sometimes they walk backwards, or roll head-over-heels forwards, or roll sideways at surprising speed, or drag a large log or a length of heavy chain, or carry a rock on their heads.

The 'subjugation of the flesh' to kill sin and impious thought is a familiar element of Christian worship. But according to Hindu scriptures, 'You cannot renounce the flesh for the sake of the soul, for both are one, and

ABOVE: Shiva sits on a throne of lotus leaves, holding a drum to represent creation and a flame, symbolising destruction

OPPOSITE PAGE: Vishnu, Lord of the Universe, in his incarnation as Krishna

what you do to the flesh you do to the soul. Kill either, kill both'. Hindu religion is no enemy to sensuality; it celebrates the erotic pleasures of the Lord Krishna, and incorporates into its temples hundreds of naked gods, goddesses and chosen maids enjoying all manner of explicitly sexual pleasures. Hindu holy men have different reasons for their apparent austerity, which spring from their ancient theology. This body of theology, as expressed in the lives and stories of Hindu gods and goddesses, is so vast and complicated that to claim almost anything about it is to invite immediate contradiction from several differing schools of thought.

Perhaps the best way to tackle the labyrinth of Hindu characters and beliefs is to become familiar with just a few of the gods and goddesses, all manifestations of the One Light, and with some of the practices followed by their worshippers.

Hindu deities

Brahma, the Creator, sent forth the principle of the universe: that from the acts performed by all beings in this universe. the chain of cause and effect is established, until all things material and spiritual returned to the bliss of Nirvana in him as the one spiritual essence.

Saraswati, his consort and sexual companion, is brighter than the light of 10 million moons. She is the mother of the sacred scriptures, the embodiment of nature and patroness of the arts – of which the art of love is the most important and valuable. She is exceedingly beautiful, always smiling, and her

ABOVE: the Temple of Somnath in Gujarat, India: one of the 12 most sacred Shiva temples in the Hindu world

whole body is elaborately decorated with precious jewels and pearls.

The five senses are sacred to Brahma and Saraswati: eyes, ears, nose, mouth and skin – we must use them all in life to understand the spiritual, with ultimate understanding coming from the sexual orgasm in which all the senses are involved to their utmost.

Shiva is pure existence, pure consciousness, god of the mind, the Lord of the Dance, Master of the Three Worlds, the Conqueror. He is often portrayed armed and with three eyes: the third eye gives him inner vision and can destroy anyone on whom it looks.

Kali, Shiva's consort and his sexual companion, is the Liberator to those who know her as she is, but the Dark and Terrible One to those who can only see her as a destroyer. She is time, space, air, fire, water and earth, and the possessor of the 64 sexual arts with which she increases the joys of Shiva. The Kama Sutra is her sacred scripture. 'Here in my body', sings the devotee of the goddess Kali, 'are the sacred rivers; here are the sun and the moon and the stars, as well as all places worthy of pilgrimage. There is no other temple as blissful as my own body.'

To Hindus the physical body is seen as the temple of the soul, the microcosm of the universe, with gardens of delights, rivers, sanctuaries and the Nine Gates, or entrances. It must be kept clean, healthy and harmonious with the wishes of Shiva and Kali.

Vishnu, the Preserver, Lord of Waters, maintains all things. He is Lord of the Universe, and in his incarnation as Krishna is the embodiment of the ardent young lover.

Lakshmi, his consort and sexual companion, is as beautiful as 10 million rising suns, and is the embodiment of sensuality. She rests naked on his thighs in ecstatic vision.

Together they are eternal lovers, ever in sexual and spiritual union – which is the symbol of loss of self in the ultimate oneness of Brahma; the return to a state of unknowing, before the beginning of time and space.

Karma

Out of all this, and much else, emerges the idea of Karma. Put simply, this means that we must accept full responsibility for our own actions at all times, and be ready and willing to experience their results in our present life. Hindus go further: they believe that we have had previous lives, or incarnations, with good or bad results, and that these are still affecting us for good or ill. What we do in this life, by the same token, will have results on our future lives. Reincarnation is the process by which this working-out of personal salvation is made possible, because nobody else can do it for you. Salvation is the final deliverance from continual rebirth into a world of illusion.

Dharma

The Sanskrit word *dharma* may be translated as 'religious or moral duty'. This concept is closely linked with the Indian caste system, which many Westerners find objectionable – even though their own class structure is often as rigid and traditional. The *dharma* of a brahman, or priest, is to study, teach and to offer sacrifices. It is the *dharma* of a kshatriya, or a warrior, to fight; and it is the *dharma* of an ordinary householder to raise his family and to offer the accustomed sacrifices. The caste in which Hindus are born is the one in which they must die, because they will come to nothing if they try to avoid their *dharma*. Everybody's *dharma* can be accomplished by the recitation of the Sacred Invocations, repeating the holy name of particular gods or goddesses, visiting holy temples and performing the exercises of Yoga. In these ways, spiritual merit can be increased, and the liberation of the soul from the Wheel of Life can be brought that much nearer.

That is one reason why the holy man prostrates himself on his pilgrimage to the Temple of Shiva. As he does so, he recites some of the Sacred Invocations, repeats the holy name of a god and makes his way towards a temple, and he does all this in his capacity as a Yogi: one who follows the path of Yoga.

Yoga

Yoga is a dramatically misunderstood word in the Western world: it means both more and less than many a popular television programme or magazine article has made out. It has very little to do with the ability to walk on water or through fire, and it has very little to do with holding your breath for an hour or performing the Indian rope act. Its basic meaning is 'to join together' or 'to make union', deriving from *yuj*, the Sanskrit term which means 'to join', or 'to yoke'. This has been developed to mean the concentration of all the attention on an object, a subject or a purpose; and this, in turn, has come to mean the union of our will to the will of God, and the achievement of poise of soul, enabling the acceptance of the whole of life in all its various aspects.

The chief purpose of Yoga is to achieve the complete unity of the soul with the fully conscious action – on both physical and spiritual levels. So, for example, the Hindu holy man concentrates his entire attention on his pilgrimage, using the physical efforts of his body to make sure that the task he has undertaken – the holy journey – is the only subject of his thoughts and intentions.

The temple of Shiva which the holy man eventually reaches holds a different meaning for him from that which it holds for non-Hindus. It is, in fact, a completely different temple from the picturesque building which the tourist sees *en route* to the next sight.

ABOVE: Hindu women on the steps of the Jagdish Shiva temple in Rajasthan

LEFT: the Lord Vishnu's incarnation as the fish-god, Matsyavatara

THE BHAGAVAD GITA

HINDUISM IS A DIVERSE RELIGION with no single founder, institution, deity or holy scripture. Its earliest known religious texts are 3,000 years old, and are probably records of even older verse, handed down by word of mouth from generation to generation. Nobody knows how long this system existed before the ancient verse was finally written down.

KNOWN AS THE VEDAS, the oldest Hindu scriptures include hymns to creation, sacrificial rites and sacred chants. The later Upanishads are Sanskrit texts examining the underlying philosophy of Hinduism and reinterpreting the Vedas, with the emphasis on knowledge, understanding and spirituality, as well as action. Over 100 Upanishads exist; the most significant, the Vedanta, date from the 8th to the 4th centuries BC.

Two epic poems form another, still later, part of the Hindu canon. The Mahabharata and the Ramayana bring together traditional legends of many centuries, and were probably compiled between the 4th and 2nd centuries BC. The Ramayana, a poem of around 24,000 couplets, tells the story of the exiled King Rama, whose wife Sita is abducted by the demonic Ravana, and who sets out to win her back. Its moral is the triumph of righteousness over evil. In the Mahabharata, the world's longest poem (about 90,000 couplets), a war is waged between two rival branches of a ruling family, representing (though not always consistently) good and evil.

Of the 18 books in the epic, the Bhagavad Gita ('Song of the Lord') takes up 18 chapters, relating the discussion between prince Arjuna and Lord Krishna, the eighth incarnation of the God Vishnu, on the eve of a great battle.

ABOVE: in the court of King Rama, whose story is told in the Ramayana

The Song of the Lord

The key players in this turbulent drama are the sons of Pandu, King of Hastinapura, who takes the throne after his father's death – his elder brother, Dhrita-rashtra, being disqualified by his blindness. After Pandu's own death his five sons, Yudhishthira, Bhima, Arjuna, Nakula and Sahadeva, are taken in by Dhrita-rashtra and trained to be superb warriors. The eldest, Yudhishthira, is named heir to the throne by his uncle, arousing the violent jealousy of the blind man's own sons – a formidable brood of no fewer than 100. Arjuna is the greatest of the Pandu heroes: brave, generous, faithful and good-looking. His doubts about the morality of fighting his own cousins trigger the dialogue with Krishna, who has appeared in the form of his charioteer. In persuading Arjuna to join battle, Krishna sets out the principles that, to many Hindus, form the real core of their religious belief. First Krishna maintains that in war only the body is killed: the soul is eternal – and that of a warrior makes it straight to heaven, so Arjuna would actually be doing his relations a good turn by taking their lives. Then he argues that it is Arjuna's duty to his caste, the Kshaṭriyas (warriors), to fulfill his purpose and go to war. Krishna finally reveals himself as a god and tells Arjuna that even in battle the soul can be liberated, finding God's presence everywhere and achieving

the peace of spiritual knowledge and devotion. All worship, says Krishna, is rewarded; and all virtue is its own reward. In the final section of his Song, Krishna praises the man who does his duty, renounces desire and selfishness, pride, anger and greed, and thus finds loving communion with God: 'Give thy mind to me, and give me thy heart, and thy sacrifice, and thy adoration. This is my Word of promise: thou shalt in truth come to me, for thou art dear to me.' (trans: Juan Mascaró, Penguin Books.)

The significance of the Bhagavad Gita

The Song of the Lord gives Krishna a human face, showing him as a friend and adviser to Arjuna, as well as a god. The concept of union with a loving God as the highest goal was at the time a new one in Hinduism, and this notion, as well as the idea of salvation by many routes, has given the Gita particular appeal, especially for contemporary Hindus. Mahatma Gandhi hung verses from the book on his bathroom wall so that he could learn them as he washed; his Gujarati translation of the text made it widely accessible within the Hindu world. For Gandhi the

ABOVE: the chariot fight between Drona, the Kaurava leader, and Bhima and Arjuna, two of the five sons of Pandu

main inspiration of the Bhagavad Gita was its message of selfless work, serving others for no material gain, as a path to salvation. With this interpretation, the book played a major role in the development of a non-violent movement for Indian independence.

BELOW: King Rama worships Shiva before setting out to rescue Sita

SACRED
HINDU SITES

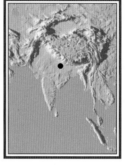

A *HINDU TEMPLE* is the dwelling-place of the deity, an earthly replica of the heavenly home. On special feast days there are gatherings of worshippers to hear recitations from the holy scriptures and to sing hymns, but most of the time the temple is regarded as the home of that temple's particular deity. Its architecture is a vision of the holy mountain on which the deities live, and its sensuous sculpture represents the bodily and spiritual delights so freely given to all believers. The deity lives there, and, just as at Roman Catholic shrines of the Virgin Mary, the image is treated as the embodiment.

The Hindu deity is woken gently every morning with tinkling bells and bathed with perfumed water. Incense is burned to provide pleasure, offerings of food and milk are made, and flowers are garlanded around the neck. Music is played and the *deva-dasis*, or temple girls, perform an erotic dance. At night the temple is closed, and the deity is left to sleep.

The life of the impoverished worshipper may be hard, but in the temple there is heaven on earth, a glimpse of pleasures to come with the deities, or in the embraces of a lover: pleasures both physical and spiritual.

Celebrations of Shiva

Sometimes, in temples sacred to Shiva, festivals are held on especially holy days, commemorating an incident from the epic of his relationship with Kali, his consort and sexual companion. The symbols and objects of special blessing and protection are the Womb-House of the temple and the *lingam*, or phallus, which is placed at the centre of veneration at most such celebrations. In small local temples it is carved from wood; in larger and richer temples it is of polished stone. In either case the phallus is about 2m high and thicker in girth than true in proportion, exaggerated to signify the potency of Shiva. Placed in the most prominent position, it is garlanded with bright orange marigolds around its shaft and dark green leaves around its base. Veneration and praise continues all day and late into the night: drums throbbing in complicated cross-rhythms, tinkling bells, a flute, the sounding of gongs and the dancing of the *deva-dasis* hour after hour, re-enacting the heroic or erotic incident from the epic. There is sometimes a pause to allow a priest to anoint the bulbous head of the phallus with perfumed oil or clarified butter, and the worshippers attend sometimes silently, sometimes clapping, sometimes singing, some standing, some kneeling, some prostrate, for hours on end.

THE CHOSEN MAIDS are the Apsaras, the Hindu equivalent of angels: girls with smiling faces, expressive hands, globular breasts, small waists, rounded bellies and wide hips, who make music, dance and, above all, embrace their worthy lovers by a great variety of exquisitely erotic techniques. The whole temple, therefore, both in function and in embellishment, is a living parable of the physical and spiritual lesson of this exalted sexual vision of life and values.

ABOVE: a priest accepts offerings from the faithful at a holy Hindu shrine

OPPOSITE: pilgrims crowd into a temple set at one of the sources of the sacred River Ganges

RIGHT: *a few of the thousands of sculptures gracing the Meenaskshi Temple, Madurai*

At Amarnath, in the northern state of Kashmir, there is a sacred cave 4,000m up the steep foothills of the Himalayas, to which, during one month of the year, 20 or 30 thousand devout Hindus come on pilgrimage. The way is long and hard, even from the nearest rough track, and the ascent is dangerous even on the best of days, but the cave is sacred to the Lord Shiva, because deep in the furthest recesses is a symbol of his special potency: the *lingam*, or phallus. This particular version is an icicle, standing about 2m high, which forms every year, though it waxes and wanes with the climate. Upon its size depends the blessing of Shiva on the

BELOW: *the towering outer walls of the temple at Madurai, busy with statues*

world: when it is large, we can expect a fruitful year to come; when small, it is a sign of Shiva's anger at the spread of evil.

Madurai Temple

The home of the deity to whom a temple is dedicated starts with a small room, called the Womb-House, just large enough to allow a ritual procession in single file around the *lingam* at its centre, circling clockwise seven times. The entrance to this room is framed with an arch incorporating depictions of loving couples, and at the base on either side are images of Ganga and Yamuna, the two river goddesses of purification. Outside the arch is a large hall, in which worshippers make their offerings; other such halls are deliberately aligned so that there is a direct view of the deity from each one.

This whole inner temple stands on a raised platform surrounded by a square or rectangular cloister with open verandas, and on special high days of festival various minor deities are carried in procession on golden carriages around these areas to the accompaniment of hymns, gongs and dancing.

A stone structure towers above, storey after storey, each with its own set of smaller and smaller halls and verandas. Everywhere there is an extraordinary abundance of carvings of gods and goddesses, chosen maids, sacred animals, fruits, flowers and vegetation.

Of all these thousands of temples, strewn across India, the most magnificent is at Madurai, in the southern state of Tamil Nadu, about 500km from Madras. It is undoubtedly one of the most truly memorable places of pilgrimage anywhere in the world.

Named after Meenaskshi, a princess who married Shiva in his incarnation as the Lord Sundareshwara, it was originally established in the 12th century, though much of the present structure was built in the middle of the 17th. Four monumental gateways lead through the massive outer walls of the main courtyard, five others into the sanctuary, all covered with sculpture. A vast multiplicity of delicately worked and coloured columns stands in the Hall of a Thousand Pillars, every one different and carved in high relief. Thousands and thousands of statues tell in stone the great epics – orange, gold, green, blue, purple, silver and black – all based on one simple theme: 'One is all, all is one'.

The structure rises in a series of roofs and domes and towers, architecture and sculpture inseparable. Crest after crest of stone echoes the ranges of mountains where the deities dwell, a lotus flower, or solar halo with sun-rays, crowning the four sides of the last roof, to indicate the passage into Heaven.

In January or February of each year, the actual date depending on the seasons of the Hindu liturgical year, there is a festival called Teppam, when images of the god Shiva, in his incarnation as the Lord Sundareshwara, and his wife, the Lady Meenasakshi, are taken in triumphal procession from the temple and floated on huge decorative rafts to an island in a vast artificial lake. Shops and stalls sell food and drink and religious souvenirs, the temple is open day and night, and loud processions take place after dark, with flickering candles, gongs, drums, flutes, singing and dancing, its lights reflected in the water. This exuberant and joyous occasion is probably the most popular pilgrimage of them all.

The River Ganges

From the high crags to the bend of the Bay of Bengal, sliding and wandering across the plains to be joined by the River of Yamuna, the waters of the goddess Ganga flow: the Ganges (Ganga), holy river of India. At Alla-habad, where the Ganges and Yamuna merge, the great high gods spilled the seed of immor-tality in the form of a single drop of the semi-nal fluid of Shiva, and every year, on the festival of Audh Kumbh, millions of devout Hindus assemble as pilgrims to bathe in these twice-blessed waters.

From here to the point where the Ganges is joined by the Brahma Putra, another sacred river, the banks are rich with temples and steps leading down to the waters, with the *lingam* of Shiva ever-present next to the *yoni* of Kali: male and female. Millions of men and women gather all the way to the delta, ritually

bathing, making their private devotions and chanting the Sacred Invocations.

Another custom, practised all over India, is the open-air burning of the dead, and nowhere is this more symbolically poignant than along these reaches of the Ganges: the platform, the dry wood, the body wrapped in its white cotton shroud, the garlands of farewell flowers; and then the fire, the hymns of the mourners, the heat, the ascending smoke and finally the scattering of the ashes into the river. The water, say the Hindus, is more than the reflection even of the sun on its surface. Reality is more than appearance.

Above: ritual bathing and prayer at Varanasi, India

Left: millions of pilgrims crowd into the holy city of Haridwar, set on the banks of the holy River Ganges

MAIN PICTURE: *a pilgrim makes his way along the Bhagirathi Valley on the return journey from the source of the Ganges* BELOW (TOP): *bathing in the Ganges waters* (BOTTOM): *a small gathering of mourners prepares to decorate and burn a funeral pyre*

BUDDHISM

B UDDHISM IS BASED ON the inner quest of the individual for enlightenment, or Nirvana, by means of meditation, wisdom and higher moral values. Devotees of Buddhism have their sacred places too, in the valley of the Ganges where Buddha lived and died.

Images of Buddha among yak-butter candles in Ganden monastery, near Lhasa

BUDDHIST PILGRIMAGE

Orthodox Buddhists do not make pilgrimages as Westerners would understand the term – but they do make personal journeys in search of deeper spiritual awareness; and many Buddhists visit some of their holy places in the hope of being taught or reminded of their tradition's founder and his teachings.

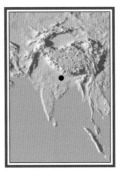

GAUTAMA, LATER TO BE known as Buddha, or the Great Enlightened One, was born to a wealthy family in a small tribal community in the north of Bengal, to the south of the Himalayas, about 550 years before the birth of Jesus.

He had every advantage of the aristocrat: he was bold and handsome, had plenty of money and nothing much to do except ride horses and hunt, play games and pass the time with girls; but he was bored and frustrated.

Gautama married a beautiful cousin when he was 19 and tried to settle down – but he was dissatisfied with the fleeting nature of worldly happiness, and was reminded increasingly on every hand of disease and death.

He then met a wandering holy man, or Yogi, who claimed to be seeking a deeper reality, and persuaded Gautama to give up everything for the life of the spirit – which, as with so many of these systems, meant subduing the lusts and pleasures of the flesh. That very day, Gautama's wife gave birth to a son. He went softly to where she slept, surrounded with flowers, with their baby in her arms, resisted the craving to take up the child in one first and last embrace, turned away, sacrificing all that he valued, and then rode off to a life of self-denial.

Gautama cut off his hair with his sword, removed all his jewels and sent everything back to his wife. Then he exchanged fine clothes for the filthy rags of a beggar, and considered himself free to search for wisdom. He lived with hermits and teachers and gave himself up to terrible austerities and self-punishment: legend has it that he existed on one hour of sleep and one grain of rice a day.

Early one morning, reduced to a skeleton, Gautama fainted from weakness when trying to meditate. He recovered, but suddenly understood that whatever wisdom a man may reach is best reached by a living soul in a living body.

Then came the Great Enlightenment: Gautama sat to eat under a magnificent fig-tree by the side of a river, and had a vision. After sitting there all day and all night in profound thought, he rose to walk to the holy city of Benares, to teach men what he had been shown about the Way of Truth. Inevitably, the story has been embellished with legends and mysteries, and some will have it that the Prince of Evil showered the world with a thousand appalling meteors at that very moment; that rivers flowed back towards their sources; that the mountains crumbled to the earth, and that the sun enveloped itself in awful darkness, and a host of headless spirits filled the air – but Gautama walked on towards Benares, undeterred. Once in Benarcs, a fanatically religious city, Gautama was eventually able to persuade 60 or so people to join him, and he and they gradually evolved a new teaching about the spiritual life.

Buddhist teachings

Writing had not yet spread to India, and ideas had to be transmitted by word of mouth. Gautama wisely framed the new message under easily memorised headings known as the Four Truths: suffering is inherent in life, and must be accepted; all suffering is caused by selfishness; suffering ceases when desire ceases; and until we overcome desire, we will have sorrows. These desires take three main forms, all of which are evil: first, the gratification of the senses; secondly, the

desire for personal salvation or immortality; and thirdly, the greed for possessions. All these must be overcome before life can be serene – so we must cease living for ourselves. When the self, or ego, has withered from the inner life, one has reached detachment – the higher wisdom, serenity or spiritual bliss.

Gautama did not believe that this was total extinction, the complete loss of self in God, but merely the rejection of those desires that necessarily render life futile.

Despite the simplicity of Gautama's message, the disciples started to modulate it into a closed system with a set of dogmas and doctrines: a church.

Stories developed of Buddha having fasted for 49 days in the wilderness; it was said that the Spirit of Evil tempted him to turn the Himalayas into gold, that he performed 32 healing miracles and was transfigured into a being of light in the presence of

LEFT: a Nepalese gilt-copper figure of Buddha

IN RUDYARD KIPLING'S *Kim* (1901), a Tibetan lama is making a pilgrimage to the holy places where the blessed feet of Buddha have trodden, thus hoping to acquire merit and free himself from the Wheel of Life. He and the boy, Kim, walk the roads and tracks of India, asking everywhere for the River of the Arrow. It seems that when Gautama was about to marry his cousin, he was accused of being too weak and tender for marriage and undertook a triple trial of strength. During one trial, the trial of the bow, he shot an arrow out of sight; when it finally fell to earth a stream appeared where it landed, which presently became a river that could wash away all sin. In the novel the lama, knowing that he is near his last death, sits under a tree by a brook meditating for two days and two nights, until his soul breaks free of his body. But at the moment of spiritual triumph a voice calls to him to return for the boy's sake. The lama drags himself back from his hard-earned bliss, staggers to his feet and tumbles into the brook: the River of the Arrow.

RIGHT: a Tibetan banner illustrates the Buddhist goal of higher wisdom, or spiritual enlightenment

BELOW: a Buddhist recites his devotions with the help of a prayer wheel, which spins to activate prayers and make them effective

his disciples; that he fed 500 people with one small cake, and that on the day of his death in his 80th year there was an earthquake.

Gautama's philosophy was naturally limited by the existing ideas of his time, and these were of perpetual cyclic recurrence, of reincarnation in what has been called a 'stagnant circling' of the universe for all eternity. The prospect can be so daunting and remote that even escaping from it can cease to be of any importance. But Buddha's Eightfold Path has inspired millions who do not profess to be Buddhists. This holds that we must have 'right views' – a rejection of unworthy acts and cruelty, with no place for unexamined beliefs or superstitions. We must have 'right desires' for all the good things: the service of others, an insistence on justice, the need for personal peace and social and racial harmony. 'Right speech' is plain and truthful, gentle and soothing, with no swearing or obscenity. 'Right conduct' involves showing courtesy and consideration for all and abstaining from killing any living being, including animals. 'Right livelihood' means harming nobody by the work that one does and giving attention to one's own health and the proper balance between body and soul. 'Right effort' is hard work, rather than merely having big plans and good intentions – but not so hard that rest is lacking. 'Right mindedness' is the constant guard against conceit, selfishness and blind stupidity. Finally, 'right rapture' is the discernment of what is genuine about religious experience – especially the danger of what appears to be spiritual ecstasy – and knowing when full enlightenment has truly been achieved.

The religion without God founded by Gautama was one with no theology, no temples, no sacrifices or priests, no sacred places, no sacred books and not even a Buddha. But even before he died it had been misunderstood and corrupted, usually with the best motives. The idea of removing desire and renouncing the self soon moved to the idea of suppressing desire and renouncing the active life. Although Gautama insisted on the Eightfold Path for its own sake, his disciples, like

many priests, introduced fear as a persuasion, and reintroduced the ideas of Hell as eternal torment. Very soon, with obvious elements and variations of Hinduism, there was a church and a sacred book, the Three Pitakas.

Buddhism today

The two main branches of Buddhism have their roots in the movement's earliest days. Theravada Buddhists believe that salvation only comes to those who adhere strictly to an austere life under their interpretation of Buddha's code. Mahayana Buddhists see salvation as open to everyone, and introduced the concept of the personal guide, or *bodhisattva* – one who has found enlightenment but chooses to stay in the world to help others. Many other schools have developed in various countries and have taken on features of their own religions: Zen Buddhism, for instance, absorbed elements of Taoism after spreading to China (see pages 172–4).

Buddhist temples are undoubtedly some of the most beautiful in the world: large, simple and profoundly impressive, but they are almost completely dedicated to the monks and priests in whose hands they are. With permission, visitors may attend services and watch rituals – but not to take part: what they do is for their own spiritual progress.

ABOVE: Buddhist monks gather to chant at a spectacular sacred site in Myanmar (Burma)

THE
PALI CANON

WHEN BUDDHA DIED (see pages 158–61) he left no heir, no successor and no scripture to lead his followers. His advice to those seeking guidance was simply to look to his teachings, or his *dharma*. Before long, several different schools of thought about these teachings were developed, prompting calls for a unified, 'authorised' version of Buddha's word.

IT WAS DECIDED THAT A meeting should be summoned to bring together Buddha's disciples and to reach a consensus about the Buddhist message. The first council of Buddhists is generally agreed to have been at Rajagha in about 483 BC, during the monsoon season. Here, the monks and nuns of the Buddhist community eventually settled on a code of monastic regulations – the *vinaya-pitaka* – and a definitive version of the Buddha's discourses – the *sutta-pitaka*.

Included in the *sutta-pitaka* ('Basket of Teachings') are 547 stories and parables illustrating Buddhist principles and describing the life of the Buddha in previous incarnations. One such tale is of a thief who tries to rob the Buddha, intercepting him on his journey and ordering him to stand still. The Buddha continues on his way, pointing out that he is still, in spirit, whereas the robber, though physically rooted to the spot, is moving all the time in his hatred and covetousness.

BELOW: the Buddhist wheel of life, painted on a wall in Ladakh, India

A popular collection of the Buddha's sayings falls into this *pitaka*, too. Known as the Dharmapada ('Verses on *dharma*'), it consists of 423 verses – such as: 'Conquer the angry man by love; conquer the ill-tempered man by goodness; conquer the miser with generosity; conquer the liar with truth'. Another describes the necessity of ruling a wayward mind: 'As the arrow-maker whittles/And makes straight his arrows,/So the master directs/His straying thought.'

Although there was not unanimous assent to the body of work established at the first council, the *vinaya-pitaka* and *sutta-pitaka* were memorised and passed on by word of mouth. A hundred years later a second council was held, at Vesali, to iron out differences about the code of monastic discipline. In the final version of the *vinaya-pitaka* ('Basket of Discipline') three aspects of Buddhist community life were tackled: the rules of conduct for monks; those for nuns; and rules concerning particular topics such as dress, food and holy occasions.

At the third council, called by King Ashoka at Pataliputta in 253 BC, nine months of work was put in by a thousand monks to check and classify the Buddhist teachings that had been recited down the generations since the Rajagha gathering. A third 'basket' was now added to the first two: the *Abhidhamma-pitaka*, or 'Basket of Higher Teachings', seven books of esoteric commentary on Buddhist doctrine, to aid meditation.

Written texts

Not until 400 years after the original synod were the Buddhist traditions collected in written form. The scriptures were compiled in Sri Lanka in the 1st century AD and written in one of the ancient Indian languages, Pali. Known as the Pali canon or *tipitaka* ('Three Baskets'), this is still held by Theravada Buddhists in Sri Lanka, Myanmar (Burma), Cambodia, Laos and Thailand to be the authoritative version of Buddhist teachings. Theravada monks still chant in the Pali language, rather than Sanskrit, and the *tipitaka* is still studied as their central Buddhist text. A vast range of other writings is studied and produced by various schools in Japan, Tibet, China and other parts of the world, reflecting the diversity of the Buddhist movement. Divisions within the community became apparent soon after the Buddha's death. Different interpretations of his sayings and disagreements over the hundreds of rules governing the monastic community's life were the cause of much debate, even after the establishment of an authorised code. The Buddha's teachings, by their very nature, resisted the constraints of institutionalised organisation, and encouraged the development of new traditions, such as the Mahayana, a name applied to several schools based around the Buddha's word that began to emerge hundreds of years after his death. Within this tradition the new concept was introduced of a *bodhisattva*: an enlightened being who refuses to pass into Nirvana but who stays in the world in order to help others find enlightenment. Mahayana texts include the Guide to Perfect Wisdom (*Prajna-paramita-Sutra*), which sets out to explain the state of enlightenment, as well as the *tipitaka* and several other works.

LEFT: fresco in the Temple of the Tooth, Kandy
BELOW: a figure of Buddha in a temple in Colombo, Sri Lanka

SACRED BUDDHIST SITES

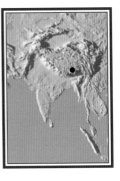

PILGRIMS TO ALL kinds of Buddhist shrines or holy temples time their journeys so that their arrival will fall on one of four significant days of each month. These four days mark the four phases of the moon, and of the four the day of the full moon is by far the most auspicious for Buddhists. At the sacred site, a bunch or arrangement of flowers is offered, some food is given as alms to the monks or nuns in charge, a small oil lamp representing wisdom and enlightenment is lit and incense is burned to symbolise purity. These are the customs generally followed; after this the procedure depends on the individual's preference. One pilgrim might, for example, repeat the

Five Precepts: no killing, no stealing, no lying, no sexual misconduct and no drinking of alcohol; another may choose to repeat some favourite sentences from the *Sayings of the Buddha*, or perhaps recite the tenets of the Eightfold Path. In keeping with Buddhist philosophy, there is no fixed ritual or order of service.

Potala Palace

Before the brutal Chinese invasion and occupation of Tibet in 1951, thousands of pilgrims would make the long and dangerous journey to the holy city of Lhasa, where, on

THERE ARE LITERALLY thousands of Buddha images all over Asia, some in series, some in solitary meditation, following several main themes. The Buddha may be recognised by posture, in one or other of his manifestations: sitting in the cross-legged Yoga position of the Lotus, he is Buddha the Meditator, in whose enlightenment we may share; standing, he is the Buddha active as a teacher in the world, in whose work as a bringer of peace we have the privilege of joining by our example; reclining, he is the Buddha who gives rest at the end of our labours and last life. He may also be the healing or life-giving Buddha, and so on, into the less easily accessible regions of symbolism. Some say the various gestures of the hands, each with a different significance, are as many as the days of seven years.

Left: a golden image of Buddha in Potala Palace

ABOVE: the 8th-century teaching temple of Borobudur in Java

BELOW: one of the circular terraces at Borobudur, representing spiritual life

top of the Potala, or 'Buddha's Mountain', was the largest Buddhist monastery in the world and the palace of the Dalai Lama, their reincarnated spiritual leader.

In that vast, 13-storey building, built in the 17th century, there were over 100 chapels, 10,000 shrines and 20,000 statues, gold and silver by the ton, stupendous tombs, mural paintings and, in the Jokhang Temple, an enormous jewel-encrusted statue of Buddha. Buddhism in Tibet was repressed by the Chinese during the cultural revolution and few of its original monasteries remain.

Borobudur

The largest Buddhist temple in the world is at Borobudur, in what used to be Java but is now Indonesia. Borobudur means 'many Buddhas'; the temple was built to hold statues

of Buddha, each in a slightly different posture or with hands held in a different ritual gesture, illustrating various aspects of his teaching. This was a 'teaching temple', delivering the Buddhist message in visual form.

The whole gargantuan structure, all the more impressive for being built on top of a steep hill, represents the Mount Meru of Indian mythology: the soaring peak of pure gold on which the whole universe rests in balance. There are five lower terraces, each four-square to represent the material earth. Higher up the holy mountain there are three circular terraces representing the realms of the spirit. The pilgrim, in the search for enlightenment, first climbs a long and steep flight of stone steps from the actual earth to the terraces representing the material world. A processional route is then followed around each terrace, always turning right to keep in harmony with the flow of spiritual power, then up the next flight of stairs, and so on, up and around for 5km, passing wall after wall of dramatic stone carvings in relief depicting incidents in the life of Buddha – over 1,500 or more panels. Hundreds of others depict scenes of everyday life:

LEFT: sightseers outnumber the pilgrims at Todaiji Temple in Nara, Japan

farming, hunting, musicians and dancers, wild and domestic animals and even exponents of the martial arts devised by early Buddhist monks as self-protection.

On the upper, spiritual terraces there are rows of bell-shaped shrines, in each of which is a seated Buddha, with the hands held in a different ritual gesture: prayer, meditation, welcome, blessing, peace, invitation, supplication, the granting of wishes – one finger altering the meaning, either hand holding eternity.

At the very top, in the centre of the highest terrace, is the final shrine, the Shrine of the Lotus: the ultimate achievement of Nirvana, the last death and passage into one life.

Statues and paintings

Most statues of Buddha are gigantic and overwhelmingly impressive. The Great Buddha in the Todaiji Temple at Nara, not far from Kyoto and Osaka in Japan, is set in the huge Public Gardens which were once for the exclusive use of the Emperor. This is the largest statue in the country, probably in the world. Set up in the middle of the 8th century, it is cast in bronze, weighs over 400 tons and is 16m high. The Buddha is seated and has his right hand raised in a gesture of blessing which bestows spiritual peace, while his left hand rests in the 'granting of right wishes' position.

Pilgrims come here in twos and threes, or alone, as distinguished from the coach-loads of toursits. They approach through the hall, as impressive in size as the statue itself, stand a

BELOW: the Great Buddha of Todaiji Temple towers over his visitors

few steps behind a wooden rail, give a formal bow and then look up into Buddha's serene face. Eventually, they bow again, back away from Buddha and take their leave.

In complete contrast to the size and magnificence of the Great Buddha is the much smaller image in the Chuguji Convent, also at Nara Public Gardens, which conveys an altogether less remote aspect. This is a limewood carving of the seated Buddha, which is kept in its special chapel – so all pilgrims must ask the nuns' permission to see it. An offering obviously eases the way, but is not strictly necessary. The pilgrims are then accompanied into the uncluttered chapel, where a nun draws aside a saffron curtain to reveal a young and graceful figure, with an intimate rather than an imposing air, the right hand raised lightly to the smiling face, the whole attitude one of complete awareness and friendly sympathy. As the figure is unveiled, the nuns, who contemplate Buddha's image here every morning and evening of their lives, bow with as much joy as any pilgrim.

In India, up a pass through the Vindhya Hills of Hyderabad, a series of Buddhas is painted on the inner walls of a monastery and temple cut into the rock. Buddhist pilgrims and art lovers alike are drawn to this secluded and remote place, which is now preserved and protected by the Indian authorities. The approach road has been opened up to give access to cars and coaches, but the inner world of the caves themselves, along the curving Ajanta Gorge, with the river splashing far below, is as serene as it ever was.

The outside rock-wall of the gorge is cut and carved with arched entrances and narrow windows, each decorated with a variety of manifestations of Buddha – flowers, fruit and leaves. Like Borobudur, this is a teaching temple, and the caves inside glow with paintings representing episodes of Buddha's life: horses and elephants pass by in procession, more flowers bloom, gold gleams and jewels sparkle; Buddha himself sits enthroned on the lotus while princesses sing and dance for him, and he smiles and gives his blessing.

BELOW: the ancient caves of Ajanta Gorge in India

SRI LANKA

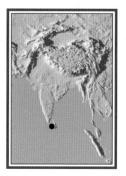

SEAFARERS OF the ancient Arab world gave Sri Lanka, the 'Pearl of the Orient', the name Serendib. From this word came the 18th-century English term 'serendipity', meaning the facility of making happy and unexpected discoveries by accident. In the search for pilgrimage sites, Sri Lanka is indeed a happy and unexpected discovery, where many different deities are worshipped with little racial or religious conflict.

The shrine of Kataragam

In the mountainous jungles about 75km east of Colombo, the almost conical Adam's Peak rises steeply over 2,500m. Thousands of pilgrims climb this mountain: the last few hours of the climb can be achieved only on foot, with the help of frequent pauses at refreshment stalls. At the very top is an enclosure, several small buildings and a large, flat boulder with an indentation. Buddhists call this the Place of the Sacred Footprint because Buddha once stood there teaching his Way. Hindus know it as the place where the Lord Shiva danced the Dance of Creation, and believe the footprint to be his. To Muslims it is the place where Adam first set foot on earth, and Roman Catholics say that the footprint is actually that of St Thomas, the Doubting Thomas of the gospels, who is known to have preached in south India during the 1st century. Pilgrims come here in crowds to worship and make offerings, most during July and August, though the temples are full of devotees all year.

The deity most often associated with Kataragam is the Hindu god known as Skanda. Buddhists come to pay homage at a shrine a kilometre away, where Buddha sat in meditation on his third visit there; Muslims come to pray at the Mosque of Masjad-ul-Khizn. But the true believers in all three faiths make offerings of food and flowers at this Hindu temple, and make their common supplications to the One who is All.

BELOW: a Sri Lankan image of Buddha's face

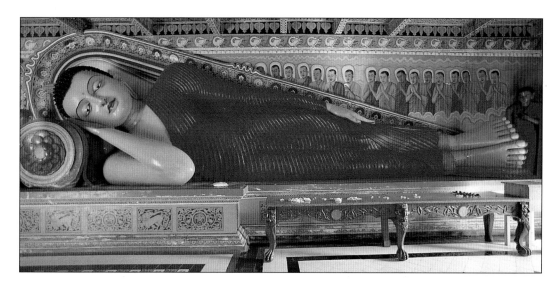

LEFT: a recumbent Buddha at the temple of Issurumuniya in Anuradhapura, where enlightenment was granted to him under a tree

RIGHT: the Passion Play held by Christians in Sri Lanka and attended by Buddhist, Muslim and Hindu believers

Negombo

About 30km north of Colombo, on the island of Duwa, is a large Roman Catholic church in the Portuguese colonial style which, throughout the Christian holy week (Palm Sunday to Easter) puts on a moving Passion Play. This is a curious mixture of traditional Asian puppets and living theatre, prose dialogue and highly ritualised song-drama, and much of the action takes place in the streets around the church. Although mostly attended by tourists and Christian pilgrims, it is also watched by many Buddhists and Muslims, and even Hindus.

The Weherehena

This Buddhist teaching temple near Matara is probably the most remarkable in the world. It has the usual impressive images of Buddha in various manifestations, but it also has a large underground Shrine Room, its walls and ceilings lined with paintings illustrating the life of Buddha from his birth to his last death. These visual aids for the illiterate, offering seeing as a way of understanding, are the equivalent of medieval Christian paintings in churches. Thousands come to see and to be taught.

The Kachchimalai Mosque

Set on a rocky headland along the beaches about 75km south of Colombo, Kachchimalai Mosque is the most famous Muslim shrine of all Asia, where thousands make a pilgrimage (second in importance only to Mecca) at the end of Ramadan, the month of fasting. Non-Muslims are not allowed to take part, but they are made welcome to the open-air feast on the beaches afterwards.

The Sacred Tree

The tree under which Gautama sat when he was granted enlightenment is known as the Sri Maha Bodhi and is found at Anuradhapura. It was grown from a cutting of the original tree (see page 158), and is undoubtedly the oldest historically documented tree in the world. Its branches are supported by iron pillars and it is surrounded by a low wall and gold-plated railing and festooned with fluttering prayer-flags and banners. It was already a venerated site for millions of Buddhists when Jesus was a young man.

The Temple of the Tooth

Several Buddhist objects of veneration are found on Sri Lanka, including hairs from Buddha's head, his wooden begging-bowl and his collar-bone, supposedly snatched from the flames of his funeral pyre. All are suitably enshrined and revered. But the most important and precious relic, a pilgrimage to which means as much to a Buddhist as Mecca does to a Muslim, is preserved at the great city of Kandy in central Sri Lanka.

BELOW: pilgrims at the Dalada Maligawa, the Temple of the Tooth

Standing alone on the shore of an artificial lake in the heart of the city is a moated pink building: the Dalada Maligawa, Temple of the Tooth, where Buddha's left canine tooth is treasured. This tooth was brought to Sri Lanka four centuries before Christ, and has, ever since, been the country's most prized possession, considered to be the very seal and guarantee of its sovereignty.

The tooth's authenticity was once doubted and an overlord went so far as to try burning it in a dish of glowing charcoal. But the charcoal, by all accounts, rose up in the form of a lotus. He had it hammered – but the hammers broke. Eventually the overlord was convinced that the tooth was genuine.

Few people, even its custodian monks, ever get to see the tooth: only the golden reliquary is on view. This is the outer casket of seven, with six increasingly smaller shrines inside, all of pure gold, and decorated with sapphires and rubies. On those rare occasions when the tooth is exposed for special reverence and veneration, it rests in a loop of gold that rises from the heart of a golden lotus.

At early morning, midday and dusk, hundreds of visitors stand briefly in the Hall of Beatific Vision in the temple, and view the reliquary in its inner sanctuary.

The Perahera, or Procession of the Tooth, is one of the most splendid and spectacular pageants in the world. It lasts a whole week in mounting fervour (the dates vary from year to year), with a vast procession through the streets every evening in four successive columns, one for each of the local deities, eventually merging into a body of priests, drummers and dancers in embroidered cloth-of-gold finery. Huge golden chariots and decorated carts carry the deities, pulled and pushed by lines of men and escorted by magnificently attired elephants in scarlet, silver and green. The main bull-elephant, with gold-tipped tusks, carries the illuminated howdah with the golden reliquary beneath a silver dome, followed by more priests, drummers and dancers. This controlled frenzy passes all night through enormous crowds, among lights, incense and perfumed flowers, watched by the followers of many faiths.

BELOW: the Temple of the Tooth, in Kandy

CHINA AND JAPAN

ABOVE: the Taoist symbol of yin and yang, the opposite and equal forces of life

*T*HERE ARE historical links between Chinese and Japanese religion. Buddhist-influenced ideas from China were imported into Japan during the 5th and 6th centuries BC. But over the centuries each of the nations has developed its own quite distinctive religious culture.

Confucius, or K'ung Fu-tzu

with a population of 1.2 billion, it has a bewildering array of faiths: Buddhism, Christianity, Animism – but none which is essentially Chinese. It does, however, have powerfully influential and ancient systems of belief: Confucianism and Taoism.

Chinese religion

Some people maintain that China has no religion of its own, in the sense of a system of belief based on a divine spirit. A vast country,

CONFUCIANISM

There are two branches of Confucian thought: one adheres to the philosophy associated with Confucius himself; the other has its roots in medieval interpretations of his thought. Confucius is the Latin form of K'ung Fu-tzu, the name of an aristocratic but poor philoso-

RIGHT: rooftops of a Confucian shrine

OPPOSITE PAGE: a torii, or sacred gate, at the Taisha shrine in Japan

RIGHT: *a peasant woman burns incense at a Taoist shrine in southern China*

pher who was born in 551 BC. After entering the civil service in the state of Lu, Confucius gathered together a following of young men, most of whom were being trained for government careers. Confucius became a successful minister but after a quarrel with the ruler he left to wander the country with his disciples.

After his death in 479 BC his teachings were collected as the *Confucian Analects.* Over the centuries other works and aphorisms were attributed to him, combining to form the 'Confucianist' school which probably has little connection with his original thought. This is a school of formal codes of behaviour, emphasising kindness (*jen*), respect and reciprocity (*shu*).

Mencius (Meng Tzu), born in about 371 BC, also worked as a government official, in the state of Chi. He, too, became an itinerant philosopher, preaching reform and peace in an age of continuous internal warfare. Mencius believed that the Confucian virtues were an integral part of human nature and could be revealed through the practice of meditation and a sense of morality; love of mankind, he asserted, should start with love of one's family and near community.

TAOISM

The Way, or Tao, was at the heart of Confucian thought; it also forms the central element of the Taoist school, a mystical philosophy based on the 4th- to 3rd-century BC texts the *Tao Te Ching,* the *Chuang Tzu* and the *Lieh Tzu.* Its main emphasis is on the communing of humanity with nature; later developments in Taoism drew on magic and *yin* and *yang,* the opposite and balancing forces of life.

Chinese pilgrimage

Symbolic rituals were developed after the death of Confucius, involving the wearing of appropriate clothes for particular occasions and the punctilious observance of ancestor worship; there are Chinese shrines and temples dedicated to Buddha; and Taoism has its own formal services. All three schools will join in ceremonies of worship or dedication. But there are no specific pilgrimages organised to holy places in their names.

There is, however, a form of private pilgrimage which is distinctively Chinese. The ancient philosophies of China have in common a profound feeling for the spirit of nature, and respect for the sense of ceaseless change – whether it be slow, as in the millions of years of geological formation, or swift, as in the waters of a stream. So men and women often make small pilgrimages to view a cloud-shrouded mountain, or a rocky gorge plunging with jade-green water, or to see the moon rising between the branches of a peach tree, or a delicate landscape reflected in a lake. This is not mere sightseeing: these pilgrims of nature are totally absorbed and made one in the contemplation of nature and of The Way.

RIGHT: pilgrims drink sacred water at the Naiku shrine in Ise, Japan

Japanese religion

Shinto, or the Way of the Gods, was once the national religion of Japan, though it lost its official status in 1945 and has not been as prevalent since the end of the war. It has no formal theology and very little systematic doctrine; its moral code owes a lot to Confucianism and something to Buddhism. Yet it has been a source of profound inspiration in

ABOVE: this elaborately decorated Chinese shrine honours the spirit of a dead ancestor

LEFT: mountains in Guilin, China – one of the magical landscapes often contemplated by the pilgrims of nature

Japan, and it induced the fervent dedication of the *kamikaze* pilots of World War II, who preferred suicide to surrender and shame.

Shinto was given its name in the 8th century, to acknowledge its difference from Buddhism. It incorporates a range of ancient beliefs, particularly the worship of nature, which emerges in the rituals of appealing to the spirits of nature (*kami*) for protection. According to Shinto belief, the Japanese emperor was a descendant of the sun god – hence the degree of devotion and duty offered by his subjects. Occupying forces after the war forbade the teaching of Shinto in an attempt to break this adherence to imperial divinity; but history shows that no religion can be suppressed that easily.

Shrines (*jinja*) to Shinto deities were built for the worship of the local *kami* and entered through the sacred

gateway, or *torii*. This symbol of Shinto is still to be seen everywhere: two upright posts, slanting a little towards each other and joined overhead by two cross-beams, the upper slightly longer than the lower, and projecting on each side of the uprights in gentle curves. *Torii* give access not only to formal shrines, but to sacred places such as groves of trees, ascents to mountains or views of waterfalls.

Shinto services, rituals, ceremonies and dramas are now private rather than state affairs. Worshippers

ABOVE (LEFT): the A-Bomb Dome (RIGHT): commemorative gifts
MAIN PICTURE: Mount Fuji and Lake Ashi

come to make offerings, perform purifications and get married or buried. These spiritual journeys are the only form of pilgrimage associated with Shinto, but they still form a significant part of everyday Japanese life.

HIROSHIMA

At 8.15am on 6 August 1945 half of the population of Hiroshima city, in San-Yo Region, was killed by the first atomic bomb used in war. Pilgrims of all faiths come to the rebuilt city to visit monuments to past and present victims of the atrocity. One of the most vivid memorials of the suffering and devastation caused by the bomb is the twisted ruin of the Industrial Promotion Hall, now known as the A-Bomb Dome; but most pilgrims pay their respects and pray or meditate in the centre of the city, at the Peace Memorial Park. Here a pale, blue flame burns before the Memorial Cenotaph, where the names of the dead are preserved in a box beneath the arch.

In the Peace Memorial Museum and Peace Memorial Hall the terrible facts are recounted, so that no one may forget or underestimate the effects of war. And around the Statue of the A-Bomb Children, thousands upon thousands of paper cranes are placed by children in memory of one victim: Sadako, a little girl who died of radiation poisoning. For Sadako, hopes of recovery depended on completing her task of folding 1,000 paper cranes. When she died she had completed 964; and now young pilgrims offer their own simple gifts in her memory.

ANCIENT SHRINES

ANCIENT CIVILISATIONS VIEWED their deities rather differently from the living religions of today. Their gods had moods and human-like emotions which affected everyday life in a tangible way. Angry gods sent storms and hardships; appeased gods would ensure prosperity. These gods are worshipped no more, but many of their temples still stand, albeit in ruins, and as tourist attractions rather than places of pilgrimage.

The evocative ruins of the Temple of Apollo at Delphi

CLASSICAL DEITIES

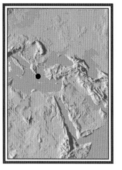

*E*DGAR ALLEN POE lamented the passing of 'the glory that was Greece'. But the glory is still there: temples, shrines and statues still stand all over the land. Only the gods and goddesses are dead. Most of their temples are admittedly in ruins, and the statues are missing heads and limbs – but their essential beauty has survived the passing centuries.

Religion in ancient Greece

The people of ancient Greece worshipped several gods and goddesses, each one associated with a particular aspect of life or place. A dozen important deities were believed to live on Mount Olympia; other, minor gods were later additions. Deities behaved in very human ways, falling in love (sometimes with

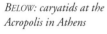

BELOW: caryatids at the Acropolis in Athens

mortals), exacting revenge, making mistakes and losing their tempers. Natural events such as storms and earthquakes were taken to be divine messages to man, and rituals and sacrifices were performed to appease or to appeal. There was no one institution or church tying the threads of Greek polytheism: priests were untrained and temples were funded by the public.

Delphi was the holiest shrine of the Greek world, home of the influential Oracle, which kings and politicians came to consult. Sacred to Apollo, god of the sun, it stood on the south face of Mount Parnassus, and was organised by a team of Delphic priests. A young girl, the *pythia*, or High Priestess, would descend into a vault beneath the main altar of the temple, where she would induce a state of mystic trance by breathing the smoke of smouldering hemp and chewing bay leaves. After this she would speak wild and whirling words in an unknown tongue. These utterances would be interpreted by her priests and were, to say the least, ambiguous. The semi-barbarian monarch, Croesus of Lydia, came to ask the Oracle whether he should make war on the growing power of Persia. Back came the response: 'You will destroy a great empire' – which, in the event, proved to be true, but the empire he destroyed was his own.

Other utterances of the High Priestess were inscribed over doors into the temple, and have passed into our common wisdom: 'Know thyself'; 'Take the middle way'.

Religion in ancient Rome

Early Roman beliefs centred around hidden spirits, or *numen*, and the spirit of ancestors and places (*genius*). New deities were adopted from Italic and Etruscan religions, and a *pontifex maximus*, or High Priest, oversaw a network of lesser priests. When Octavius took the imperial throne as Augustus, he also took the title of *pontifex* and eventually became an object of public worship. The belief that gods of all religions were the same but with different names allowed Greek deities to be fully absorbed into the ancient Roman system.

Classical sites today

Athens is an overcrowded and polluted city, but standing serene above its turmoil is the Acropolis, or 'High City', a complex of temples on a broad, flat-topped platform of limestone. Delicate marble columns support the Parthenon, sacred to the goddess Pallas Athene. Her temple has been looted of its statues, most of which are now in the British Museum in London. The structure, after years of neglect, is on the point of collapse: only scaffolding prevents the upper stones from toppling down. The marble, corroded by acid rain and car exhausts, is pitted and cracking. Yet the site's beauty still transcends modern distractions.

Delphi is one of the loveliest places in all Greece, high up on the side of the narrow valley of the Plistus river, surrounded by peaks and crags. Not much of the temple survives, and though the ruins of the sanctuary spread out across the steep hillsides, there is still a tangible majesty and mystery here. To stand in the vault below the main altar, where the Oracle's voice was heard, to evoke the presence of ancient heroes, is to be aware of unearthly powers.

ABOVE: Zeus, known to the Romans as Jupiter, and revered as the supreme god

BELOW: the Athenian treasury and Sacred Way at Delphi

DESERT AND JUNGLE

EVER SINCE the arrival of the first Europeans in Australia, its native Abo-rigine people have been regarded as barely human – despised, exploited and neglected, or seen as potential converts to Christianity. When ships first landed on Aus-tralia's shores, there were about 3 million Aborigines in all, scattered over the land in tribes and speaking about 200 languages between them. Within little more than a hun-dred years the effects of disease, ill-treatment, alcohol and land encroachment had reduced the population to 60,000. Only very recently have white Australians begun to learn about the complex culture and cus-toms that had developed among Aborigine soci-eties over many thou-sands of years.

Aborigines have an inner life of deep spiritual power, an understanding of their harsh world that most Westerners fail to appreciate. To them, the earth is sacred, their land an inheritance from the great spirits; they cannot understand why white men would abuse it for short-term profits and long-term destruction.

The central element of Aboriginal religion is the Dreamtime, or Dreaming: a period when the plants and creatures of the world emerged from land and sea and took shape, at the same time shaping their surroundings. Ever since the Dreaming, everything and everyone has been part of the same process, living to the patterns of landscape and life cre-ated at the very beginning. Aborigine lives are called the 'Dream Journey' – from one sacred place (a site of particular importance in the long story of creation) to the next, in search of food and water for the body and nourishment for their spiritual respect for the land. An ordinary day-to-day necessity is thus invested with deep significance and life becomes natu-rally religious: the world is their church.

Nearly all Aboriginal tribes were origi-nally nomadic, marking their territories and their journeys with songs and stories, passed from age to age. Life was a series of circular journeys in search of food: from sweet roots here to wild fruit there, then the eggs of migrat-ing birds elsewhere, the young green lizards somewhere further on, then the roots again – a journey complete during the natural cycle of the many Aboriginal seasons. The dances performed in gratitude for food were also the dances which taught them the ancient lessons about finding food. The songs of enjoyment at finding secret water reinforced their dependence on knowing the best places to search. Stories of their hunting forefathers would remind them of the necessity to be good hunters, and of the best ways to lure fish from the deep pools.

During any one cycle of seasons the family or tribe would cover more than a thou-sand square kilometres, following routes established over generations, from water-hole to sacred place, from a creek with fish to a cave with rock-paintings, and on to the young

BELOW: a painted path leads tourists over Uluru (Ayers Rock)

ABOVE: Uluru (Ayers Rock), one of the sacred sites on the Aborigine Dream Journey

ANCIENT SHRINES

182

green lizards. The rock-paintings, showing scenes of hunting and life and ceremonies, are perpetually alive for Aborigines, continually retouched or even repainted. Rather than historical records, they are an integral part of their faith in a way of life.

Since 1976 Aborigines in the Northern Territory have been 'granted' ownership of the lands where they were crowded into reservations by the whites. Many still find it impossible, however, to reconcile their traditional life with the pervading culture of modern Australia. But the Dreaming still lives as a powerful concept of immense practical and spiritual significance.

The Dream Journey is as liturgical in its way as the Stations of the Cross for Roman Catholics: a ritual and a form of words at each holy place, telling an old story already well known, yet new every time, filled with deep meaning and personal thought. Of course, the sites of the Dream Journey are often hundreds of kilometres apart and the cycle requires a year to complete, and is even more significant for the Aborigines as an essential part of food-gathering; as if Roman Catholics could only eat as a direct result of reciting the rosary at

each Station of the Cross. Surely no pilgrimage could be so important.

Other ancient journeys

The bushmen of the Kalahari Desert in south-western Africa have a very similar experience to that of the Australian Aborigines. Their relationship to the cycle of seasons was also as mystical as it was practical, because they travelled through a world where birds, animals, plants and people shared a common language, and where all things depended on the journey from water-hole to water-hole.

Africa has a vast collection of tribal stories about 'lost tracks' through the forest or across the desert for the spirit to follow on its last journey. Several tribes in northern Burma have complicated procedures to persuade the soul of the departed to start on its route across mountains and rivers to the unknown land.

Many other supposedly 'primitive' religious journeys are made by tribes, families, communities and cult-members, in societies all over Africa, South America, South-east Asia and the islands of the Pacific.

ABOVE: Botswana bushmen in the Kalahari Desert

ABOVE: Maori carvings

BELOW: intricate Aborigine wall-paintings in the Australian New Territories

In New Zealand some Maoris still make a conscious effort to enact the ritual canoe voyage which was once an important part of a boy's 'voyage' into manhood. Unfortunately for tradition, under the pressures of contemporary life, American television is now the greater influence, and interest has fallen away among the younger Maoris.

In New Guinea some tribes far inland from the coastal towns still teach their young people the way through the jungle to the 'land of ancestors' over the distant mountains; and the tribes of South American Indians managing to survive the loss of the tropical rain forests in the Amazon Basin talk of routes through the swamps to the hunting lands across the Great River of Death. But the loggers are draining the swamps, and with them the ways of a people, and the legends of distant mountains may disappear altogether.

Native Americans, or American Indians, were a diverse people with a rich variety of languages, customs and religions before their decimation by white settlers. Most shared the belief in a leader who would protect their communities and in a spirit of animals, who, when pleased, provided hunters with their game. Many would also re-create the universe in sacred parts of the landscape, celebrating and renewing it in their rituals.

Ancient religions and Christianity have been merged in recent attempts to revive Native American traditions, which were all but lost under the impact of white colonisers. Many Native Americans have now taken up some aspects of the old religion, and look back particularly to the 'great spirit' who characterised some faiths, and who was worshipped long before the invaders took land as their own and built their towns and temples.

S T O N E H E N G E

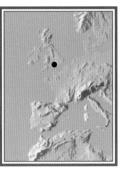

*T*HE PRACTICE of making pilgrimages to pagan holy places was already ancient in the time of the Old Testament. Although we know little about the religious customs of the prehistoric age, the massive stone circles and avenues erected by many succeeding generations living thousands of years ago still have the power to draw visitors and worshippers from all over the world.

The history

There are about 900 rings of prehistoric standing stones in Europe, dating from the late neolithic age and early Bronze Age. All are built with vast quarried slabs, some as much as 400m in diameter. The best guess of archaeologists and historians to date is that these were constructed as temples, where religious rites associated with the stars, the sun and the moon, the changing seasons and fertility were celebrated. But there is every possibility, of course, that our modern theories about these enigmatic sites are way off the mark.

Stonehenge is one of the most famous of all stone circles. It is set in magnificent natural landscape: the undulating downs of Salisbury Plain in Wiltshire, where pasture and heath, meandering valleys, streams, rivers and low hills create an open, windswept landscape under a wide sky. The plain, with its awesome

BELOW: sunset over Stonehenge

ABOVE: *Druids gather for their midsummer ceremony*

The stones themselves, probably used between 3100 and 1100 BC, were set in their inscrutable arrangement in three different phases. An earthen bank and ditch were created first, followed by the erection of two rings of 80 bluestone slabs, quarried in the Preseli Hills of Dyfed, in west Wales. It is thought these large stones were transported by raft round the coast of Wales and across the Bristol Channel, then hauled over logs to Salisbury Plain. This was later replaced with an outer circle and inner semicircle of 80 sandstone pillars.

We can only speculate about the original pilgrims and their reasons for building and returning to Stonehenge. These were people who had been hunters and nomads and were now farmers, growing wheat and barley, rear-

sense of prehistory, is at the centre of the hills and ridges of chalk that radiate over southern England and include the Downs and the Chilterns.

RIGHT: *an ancient enigma*

ing cattle and sheep, occasionally hunting for fresh meat, and fishing when they could. Their social and religious consciousness focused on menstruation, conception, pregnancy, birth, care of the sick, making fire, gathering the harvest and laying out the dead. Members of these new communities saw themselves as part of the natural world, along with earth, air, fire, water, animals, sun, moon and stars, and valued the natural cycle of life and death, growth and decay.

The earth was seen as the Great Mother, who was known by many names but whose functions and attributes were simple and elemental: her womb conceived and brought to birth all things necessary for life. Perhaps Stonehenge was associated with this relationship with the Great Mother, and with the 28-day cycle of the moon. The people who built it had a practical knowledge of the sky at night, of astronomy, geometry, mathematics and land-surveying. Stonehenge was quite possibly the central point of an observatory and calculator which recorded the seasonal movements of the sun and the cycles of the moon.

Stonehenge today

Concern for the continued preservation of these ancient stones means today they can only be viewed from behind a perimeter fence, a situation which has often caused much conflict with the authorities. But even so, Stonehenge is still a powerful magnet, drawing people from all walks of life.

THE MEGALITHIC AGE

ABOUT 7,000 YEARS AGO people began to erect massive monuments of granite and limestone in long rows, or in rings, or standing alone. These megaliths were set up, in great feats of labour and teamwork, all over Western Europe and far beyond.

MANY MEGALITHS ARE STILL STANDING: there are examples in Britain, France, Germany, Portugal, Malta, Spain and Sweden. In fact, within Europe alone, there are over 50,000 megalithic sites, legacies of thousands of years of human life that remain a mystery to the modern world.

The spread of megaliths

Megaliths began to appear during the late neolithic period, when farming and pottery production were already well-established skills and people were living in village communities. In France and Iberia the first monuments were raised in around 4500 BC; it took a further 1,300 years for the practice to spread to Britain and Ireland, and another 200 years before megalithic temples appeared in Malta. Stonehenge, altered and extended for over 10 centuries after its original construction, represents the highest peak of megalithic creativity, with vast blocks of stone and complex constructions. Later monuments were thrown up in larger numbers but on much smaller and simpler scales – such as the small round-barrow tombs across southern France.

Archaeologists have sorted the surviving monuments into four categories of megalithic architecture: stone-slab temples (such as in Malta); burial chambers, which include the dolmen (from the Celtic for 'table stone'), a horizontal slab resting on two or more vertical stones; standing stones arranged in circles or avenues (such as

Stonehenge); and single upright slabs, or menhirs ('long stones'), some of which are up to 6m high.

Burial and worship

Death rituals seem to have played a central role in many of the megalithic structures; other theories suggest

worship of an earth deity, or of ancestors, or celebrations or appeasement of natural forces. Grave offerings and human bones have been found in several burial chambers – over 100 axes and nearly 50 items of jewellery were unearthed at Mané-er-Hroech, in Morbihan, Brittany, and in other sites carbonised remains suggest that sacrificial rites may have been conducted there. In some tombs access passages seem to have been covered to hide and seal the burial section itself; and some monuments are ringed with ditches containing heaps of skeletons and offerings. In the Roaix burial vault in Vaucluse, France, 35 human skeletons had been thrown into the tomb, still pierced with the arrow-heads that killed them some time in the 3rd millennium BC.

In some areas the monuments are decorated with carved, engraved or painted patterns, whose meaning we can only imagine, though attempts have been made to interpret the frequently repeated motifs at sites in Brittany, Ireland and Portugal. Waves, spirals, broken lines and triangles may form a language of symbols relating to religious or social life; some see human representations in the abstract designs of monuments such as Barclodiad-y-Gawres ('the Giantess's Apron') in Anglesey, north Wales.

The end of an era

For over 3,000 years megaliths continued to be built and used by western communities, maybe for different purposes by different generations. But living skills and customs were changing and a new age was emerging, based on the mining and working of copper and gold. At about the same time as the Bronze Age was spreading through Europe, in the second millennium BC, megalithic culture seems to have gone into its decline. Mass burial was abandoned and individual graves came into fashion, often reserved for the powerful and wealthy, who were buried along with their weapons and jewellery. As the centuries passed the great stones were battered by the weather and pilfered by local people for new constructions. One theory suggested by archaeologists is that a new creed took the place of megalithic religion, and that its followers set out to destroy the monuments of this rival or defunct form of worship. Some tombs were adapted and used for individual burial; others were dismantled and the stone reused for tombs and coffins.

Those that survived gradually became the focus of new myths and legends. Even today, stories are still told of standing stones that grow bigger every year, or of stones that leave their sites at night and set off to the nearest river for a drink. Other popular legends tell of stone circles being the petrified forms of young women or soldiers, or of stones that dance in their rings when nobody is looking, or that groan in the dark.

Until relatively recently stones were believed to grant luck or cast spells. At Carnac, in Brittany, young girls would rub their stomachs against the stone in the hope of finding a husband; men would follow the same process at Plouarzel to make sure of strong and handsome offspring. Tales of supernatural forces, aliens and witchcraft are still spun around the megalithic sites. Their original role and purpose may be lost to us, but these monuments of a neolithic age continue to intrigue and to inspire, and to exert a power that we may never be able to explain.

ABOVE: the temple complex of Hagar Qim, on Malta, probably built in around 3000–2500 BC. The Maltese name means 'standing stones'
LEFT: Carnac, in Brittany, where girls hoping to find good husbands put their faith in the magical properties of the stone

INDEX

ACKNOWLEDGEMENTS

The Automobile Association would like to thank the following photographers, libraries and associations for their assistance in the preparation of this book.

PHOTO AKG LONDON 69a (Erich Lessing), 72a, 72b, 73 (Erich Lessing); ANCIENT ART & ARCHITECTURE COLLECTION 2, 5a, 32, 43b, 87a; ATHENS ARCHITECTURAL MUSEUM 181a; THE BRIDGEMAN ART LIBRARY 4 Lydgate and the Canterbury Pilgrims from 'Troy Book and the Siege of Thebes' John Lydgate Poetry, (British Library, London), 8 Medieval View of the City of Jerusalem (Bibliotheque Nationale, Paris), 14a & 14b Third Crusade (Bibliotheque Nationale, Paris), 15 Third Crusade (Bibliotheque Nationale, Paris), 35 St Veronica (Kress Collection, Washington D C), 45 St Catherine of Siena by Giovanni-Battista Tiepolo, (Kunsthistorisches Museum, Vienna), 69c Icon of the Virgin, Smolenskaja Monastery, Moscow (Kremlin Museums, Moscow), 71a The Black Madonna of Czestochowa (copy of the original) by Jan Krauze (Private Collection), 103 Miniature of St Brendan and a siren, St Brendan Codex (Heidelberg University Library, Germany), 110 Canterbury Tales: Nun's Priest, Ellesmere Manuscript, (Facsimile Edition) (Private Collection), 111a Canterbury Tales: The Pardoner, Ellesmere Manuscript, (Facsimile Edition) (Private Edition), 111b Canterbury Tales: Chaucer, Ellesmere Manuscript, (Facsimile Edition) (Private Collection), 111c Canterbury Tales: The Cook, Ellesmere Manuscript, (Facsimile Edition) (Private Collection), 111d Canterbury Tales: The Miller, Ellesmere Manuscript, (Facsimile Edition) (Private Collection), 119a The Round Table and the Holy Grail (detail) Roman de Tristan, (Musee Conde, Chantilly/Giraudon), 132 The mosques at Medina & Mecca, from 'Reasons for Charity', by Mustafa Al-Shukri, Persian, Literary Texts (Fitzwilliam Museum, University Museum, Cambridge), 144b Shiva sitting on a throne of lotus leaves ringed by a circle of flames holding a drum, the symbol of creation and a flame, the symbol of destruction (Victoria & Albert Musuem,London), 145 Krishna in cosmic form, Rajasthan, (Victoria & Albert, London), 149a Chariot fight between Drona, Bhima and Arjuna (Oriental Museum, Durham University), 159 Gautama the Buddha, Nepalese (gilt-copper) (Christie's Images), 160a The Paradise of Shambhala, Tibetan Banner, Musee Guimet, Paris (Giraudon), 172b Portrait of Confucius, Qing Dynasty, (Bibliotheque Nationale, Paris) ; COPYRIGHT BRITISH MUSEUM 31; E. T. ARCHIVE 39; MARY EVANS PICTURE LIBRARY 38, 38/9, 55b, 68a, 71b, 77b, 86; FIRO-FOTO 83, 92b; SONIA HALLIDAY PHOTOGRAPHS 95, 108, 112b; ROBERT HARDING PICTURE LIBRARY 1, 3d, 5b, 5c, 9a, 9b, 12, 13a, 13b, 16, 17, 18, 21a, 22a, 23a, 23b, 24a, 24b, 28/9, 30, 36, 37a, 52b, 52c, 55a, 56a, 56b, 58a, 58b, 68b, 76a, 76b, 80, 81a, 81b, 87b, 107a, 107b, 117a, 119b, 121a, 130/1, 144a, 146, 147a, 152b, 153a, 154/5, 155a, 156/7, 164, 165, 169a, 169b, 170b, 171, 172c, 174a, 175b, 176a, 182b, 183, 184a, 184b, 186; THE HULTON GETTY PICTURE COLLECTION LTD 48; THE HUTCHINSON LIBRARY 141a, 151; THE IMAGE BANK F/Cover; IMAGES COLOUR LIBRARY LTD 147b, 163a, 163b, 190; IMPACT PHOTOS 79a (M Kneale), 82 (S Parry), 88a (J Denham), 88b (J Denham), 89a (S Parry), 89b (S Parry), 90a (S Parry), 90b (J Denham), 90c (S Parry), 91 (S Parry), 92a (S Parry), 114a (D Reed), 115a (B Stephens), 117b (S Benbow), 122 (B Harris), 124c (B Harris), 138/9 (C Bluntzer), 170a (D Sansoni); KUNSTHISTORISCHES MUSEUM 37b; MAGNUM PHOTOS LTD 134a, 134b, 153b, 160/1, 166b; MIRROR SYNDICATION LTD 59, 60a, 60b; PETER NEWARK'S PICTURES 127, 128a, 128b; A & B PEERLESS 19a, 67, 70, 115b, 116a, 116b, 140b, 141b, 150, 152a, 155b, 168, 172a, 175a; POPPERFOTO 50b; REX FEATURES LTD 40/1, 41 (T Pelliot), 47a (M Setboun); PETER SANDERS PHOTOGRAPHY 133, 137; SCALA 44b, 74, 77a, 78a, 78/9, 79b, 94b, 96/7, 97a, 97b, 99; SPECTRUM COLOUR LIBRARY F/Cover inset, B/Cover, 3b, 49, 50a, 51a, 140a, 142/3, 173, 176/7; FRANK SPOONER PICTURES 46b, 47b, 51b, 52a, 61, 62a, 62b, 71c, 104/5, 104, 118, 121b, 135a, 135b, 136; TRIP 69b (M Jenkin), 148 (Dinodia/Ravi Shekhar), 149b (Dinodia/Ravi Shekhar), 162 (J Batten); ZEFA PICTURES LTD 3a, 18/9, 19b, 20, 21b, 24/5, 43a, 109, 113, 123, 124a, 124b, 129, 166a.

All remaining pictures are held in the Association's own library (AA PHOTO LIBRARY), with contributions from the following photographers:
P AITHIE 22b, 25a, 25b; A BAKER 182a, 188/9; P BAKER 114b; J BEAZLEY 125, 126c; L BLAKE 106a, 106b, 106c; D CORRANCE 166/7; P DAVIDSON 98a; P ENTICKNAP 84a, 84b, 86/7, 189; T HARRIS 3c; A HEUMISCH 100, 101a, 101b, 102a, 102b, 102c; J HOLMES 33, 167, 174b, 176b; C LEES 126a; J LOADER 11b; E MEACHER 185; D MITIDIERI 75b; I MOREJOHN 160b; D NOBLE 112a; K PATERSON B/Flap, 98b; C SAWYER 68c; A SOUTER 11a, 11c, 13c, 26, 27, 34, 42, 44a, 94a; R STRANGE 63, 64a, 64b, 64/5, 65, 66; R SURMAN 126b, 178/9, 181b; J A TIMS 53, 54a, 54b, 57; W VOYSEY 186/7, H WILLIAMS 120/1; P WILSON 75a, 180.